SECRET
NEW ORLEANS

Chris Champagne

PHOTOS
Paul Lanoue

JONGLEZ PUBLISHING

travel guides

A lifelong resident of New Orleans, **Chris Champagne** is a graduate of the Orleans Parish School system and of the University of New Orleans with a BA in History. He is a writer, performer, poet, comedian, political satirist, radio show host and columnist who has performed his work on stages all over the Greater New Orleans area.

He was voted one of 144 *New Orleans Characters* in 2012 and was voted best comedian in New Orleans in 2013 and 2014. He was a member of National Poetry Slam teams in San Francisco in 1993 and Chicago in 1999. He received artists' residencies from the Alliance of Artists in 2006 and The College of Santa Fe in 2008.

Chris is the author of the poetry book *Roach Opera* {Portals Press 2007}, and *The Yat Dictionary* {Lavender Ink, 2013}, a book on the dialect spoken by native Orleanians. His family on both sides has resided in New Orleans continuously since the first half of the 18th century.

We have taken great pleasure in drawing up *Secret New Orleans* and hope that through its guidance you will, like us, continue to discover unusual, hidden or little-known aspects of the city.

Descriptions of certain places are accompanied by thematic sections highlighting historical details or anecdotes as an aid to understanding the city in all its complexity.

Secret New Orleans also draws attention to the multitude of details found in places that we may pass every day without noticing. These are an invitation to look more closely at the urban landscape and, more generally, a means of seeing our own city with the curiosity and attention that we often display while travelling elsewhere…

Comments on this guidebook and its contents, as well as information on places we may not have mentioned, are more than welcome and will enrich future editions.

Don't hesitate to contact us:
E-mail: info@jonglezpublishing.com
Jonglez Publishing
25 rue du Maréchal Foch
78000 Versailles, France

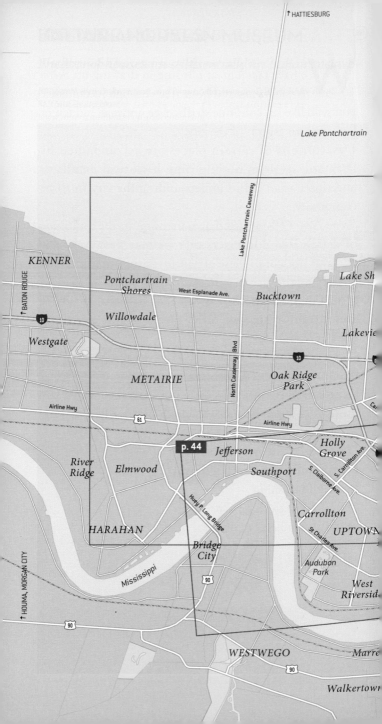

↑ HATTIESBURG

Lake Pontchartrain

Lake Pontchartrain Causeway

KENNER

↑ BATON ROUGE

10

Pontchartrain Shores

West Esplanade Ave.

Lake Sh

Bucktown

Willowdale

Lakevie

Westgate

METAIRIE

North Causeway Blvd

Oak Ridge Park

10

Airline Hwy

61

Airline Hwy

Ca

p. 44

Jefferson

Holly Grove

River Ridge

Elmwood

Southport

S. Carrollton Ave.

S. Claiborne Ave.

Carrollton

UPTOWN

HARAHAN

Huey P. Long Bridge

St Charles Ave.

↑ HOUMA, MORGAN CITY

Bridge City

Audubon Park

West Riversid

Mississippi

90

WESTWEGO

Marre

90

Walkertown

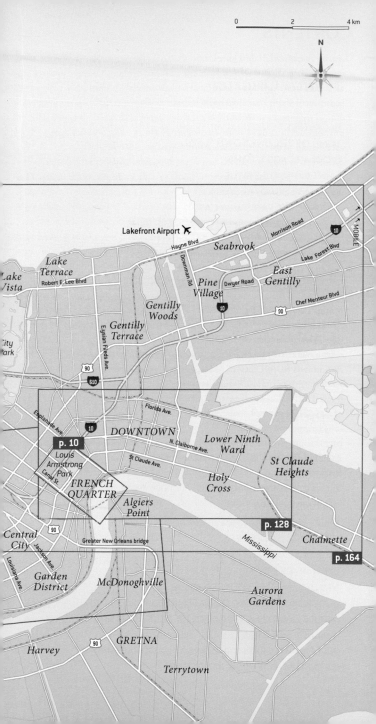

0   2   4 km

N

Lakefront Airport ✈

Hayne Blvd

Morrison Road

MOBILE

10

Seabrook

Lake Forest Blvd

*Lake
Terrace*

*Lake
Vista*

Robert E. Lee Blvd

Downman Rd

*Pine
Village*

Dwyer Road

*East
Gentilly*

Chef Menteur Blvd

90

*Gentilly
Woods*

10

*Gentilly
Terrace*

Elysian Fields Ave.

*City
Park*

90

610

Florida Ave.

Esplanade Ave.

10

DOWNTOWN

*Lower Ninth
Ward*

N. Claiborne Ave.

p. 10

Louis
Armstrong
Park

St Claude Ave.

*St Claude
Heights*

**FRENCH
QUARTER**

Canal St.

*Holy
Cross*

*Algiers
Point*

p. 128

*Central
City*

90

Greater New Orleans bridge

Mississippi

Chalmette

Jackson Ave.

p. 164

Louisiana Ave.

*Garden
District*

McDonoghville

*Aurora
Gardens*

Harvey

90

GRETNA

Terrytown

CONTENTS

French Quarter

Uptown

Downtown

CONTENTS

Lake Area

French Quarter

BACKSTREET CULTURAL MUSEUM ①

A home-made mini museum of African American culture

1116 Henriette Delille Street
Tel: 504-606-4809
www.backstreetmuseum.org - Email: info@backstreetmuseum.org
Open: Tue–Sat 10am–4pm
Entry fee: $10
#88 St. Claude-Jackson Barracks bus and #91 Jackson-Esplanade or Rampart/
St. Claude streetcar

Treme, the neighborhood next to the French Quarter that is home to Congo Square (the historical gathering place where slaves were allowed on Sundays to flex the cultures they had brought with them from Africa), is one of the crucibles of jazz and New Orleans music. And it is here you will find a home-made mini museum dedicated to the city's African American culture.

Established in 1999 by Sylvester Francis, the Backstreet Cultural Museum is a two room museum dedicated to jazz musicians, second lines, jazz funerals, Mardi Gras Indians, social aid and pleasure clubs, as well as

other aspects of New Orleans African American culture. Francis's road to becoming museum curator began when he decided, after having his picture taken for a fee in a social aid and pleasure club parade, that he would start documenting local musicians. This was followed by an encounter with Big Chief Victor Harris of The Mandingo Warriors «Spirit of Fi Yi Yi». When Francis saw the painstaking and elaborately decorated Mardi Gras Indian costume of the Big Chief discarded in the backyard at the end of the day's revelry, he salvaged it. The costume became the first item in his museum. Soon he would display other items along with his vast collection of photographs of New Orleans musicians. Mardi Gras Indian costumes, the most stunning elements of the Backstreet Cultural Museum, usually take all year to produce and are often sewn by the wearer. They are fashioned from fabric, beads, sequins and buttons, and festooned with brightly-colored feathers as their most prominent feature.

The museum is located in the heart of Treme in a former funeral home that itself was a landmark to local musicians as a place where jazz funerals used to start. It is also a living museum and meeting place for the community: you can often find artists who have contributed to the museum's collection just hanging out on site. And Sylvester or a member of his family are usually on hand to explain the unique aspects of New Orleans' African American culture and point visitors in the direction of the real thing.

TOMB OF THE UNKNOWN SLAVE ②

To all slaves who are buried throughout the United States

1210 Governor Nicholls Street
Tel: 504-525-5934
www.staugchurch.org
#91 Jackson/Esplanade bus, Rampart/St Claude Streetcar

The large cross at the side of St. Augustine Catholic Church in the Treme neighborhood, constructed from a heavy maritime chain draped with several smaller chains and human shackles, is not a common cross; it marks the spot of the Tomb of the Unknown Slave.

The place is not actually a grave in the conventional sense, but a shrine. The plaque reads: "The nameless, faceless, turfless Africans who met an untimely death in the Faubourg Treme".

Historically, Treme is a predominantly African-American section of the city across from the French Quarter. Over time, excavations for new construction or renovations to properties often turned up the bones of the deceased. It is surmised that many unknown souls were buried in this ground, including slaves, yellow fever victims and others who sometimes died in a less than an ethical manner. The brutal nature of the lives of slaves often led them to be hastily buried without even cursory protocols.

The shrine is dedicated not just to the New Orleans unknown slaves, many of whom are still believed to be buried in the ground in Treme, but to all slaves buried throughout the United States.

St. Augustine Catholic Church opened in 1841 and was built by free people of color, giving it the distinction of being the oldest African-American Catholic church in the country.

The tradition at that time was to sell pews by subscription to help finance the church. Free black parishioners also bought pews along the side of the church that were reserved exclusively for slaves to worship, along with other parishioners, both black and white. This also makes the church perhaps America's first truly integrated house of worship.

After Hurricane Katrina, the Archdiocese of New Orleans slated St. Augustine for closure along with other older parishes. The St. Augustine community rallied in defense of their church even though many of its parishioners were displaced by Katrina. With activism and passionate support from the community, the parishioners convinced the archdiocese to keep the church open.

A joint $75,000 grant from the National Trust for Historic Preservation and American Express was also instrumental in repairing the storm damage, which enabled efforts to keep this historic church open.

NICOLAS CAGE'S TOMB

Protection from transgression?

425 Basin Street at St. Louis
Tel: 504-482-5065
www.saveourcemeteries.org
Open: Mon–Sat 9am–3:30pm, Sunday 9am–12:30pm. Tour guide required to visit
#1 Cemetery #88 St. Claude-Jackson Barracks bus or Rampart/St. Claude streetcar

I n historic St. Louis #1 Cemetery, just a football field away from the French Quarter, is a white pyramid mausoleum. The tomb stands nine feet high and bears the cryptic Latin inscription *Omnia Ab Uno* (meaning 'everything from one'). Although not officially identified as such, it is widely believed among those privy to such knowledge that it was bought by actor Nicolas Cage to serve as his final resting place. Cage has had a fling or two with New Orleans; residing here for a while and purchasing both the La Laurie Mansion, purported to be the most haunted building in the city, and Our Lady of Perpetual Help Chapel. Following tax difficulties both properties were foreclosed upon in 2009. Cage obtained the tomb in 2010.

The cemetery is the oldest in the city and the resting place of some of New Orleans' most storied citizens: Paul Morphy, once the world's greatest chess player; Bernard Marigny, who developed the Faubourg Marigny area

of New Orleans and the town of Mandeville, Louisiana; and iconic Voodoo priestess Marie Laveau. This kind of eternal rest real estate is pricey and not easy to come by. Rumor, of course, runs its own narrative when celebrity is involved. Speculation abounds regarding the reasons Nicolas Cage would want to be laid to rest here in the Crescent City. One rumor claims he is associated with the Illuminati, the shadowy group some say runs the world. The pyramid is thought to be a significant symbol of the group. Another rumor alleges that Cage wanted proximity to the fabled Ms. Laveau as protection from transgressions related to his ownership of the haunted La Laurie Mansion.

New Orleans has many traditional practices; some spice up the daily exigencies of life, some simply add to its romantic reputation. One of the tried and true of these is the chalking of crosses on Marie Laveau's grave in the hope of conjuring up good luck or favors from the great beyond. With Cage's pyramid, it seems a new ritual has arisen: visitors don't need to look too hard to notice red, lip-shaped marks left by women kissing the tomb while wearing very bright lipstick.

> Cage's pyramid received a star turn of its own when it appeared in his film *National Treasure*.

SAINT EXPEDITE STATUE

Both a Catholic and Voodoo saint for those in a hurry

Our Lady of Guadalupe Chapel
411 N. Rampart Street
Tel: 504-525-1551
www.judeshrine.com
Open: Hours vary between 7am and 6pm
Rampart-St. Claude streetcar or #88 St. Claude/Jackson Barracks bus

The worshippers at Our Lady of Guadalupe Church across the street from the French Quarter on Rampart Street eagerly awaited a statue of Our Lady that was to grace the church. Alongside the expected package was a similar crate with large stenciled letters that read simply "EXPEDITE."

Opening the crate, they found a statue of a Roman soldier, sans helmet and sword, holding a palm branch in his left hand, while raising in his right hand a cross stating the Latin word *hodie* (this day). New Orleans' knack for improvisation and piousness took it from there.

Today, St. Expedite's statue graces the mortuary chapel at Our Lady of Guadalupe, the oldest church structure in New Orleans (its facade was dedicated in 1832). The church served as a funeral chapel during the many yellow fever epidemics and its proximity to St. Louis #1 cemetery leaves no doubt about St. Expedite's recruitment and eventual embrace by the city's Voodoo practitioners: these days, Expedite has the distinction of doing double duty as both a Catholic and Voodoo saint.

In all incarnations, St. Expedite is the patron saint of impatience; although 1800 years old, he is modern in the sense that he is the go-to saint for those in a hurry. He even has his own speed prayers to move things along. It is recommended that before reciting these prayers, you snap your fingers to ensure the saint's attention.

In contrast there is the Novena, a traditional nine-day prayer vigil for those in dire need of heavenly assistance. There is also a nine-hour express Novena, lovingly called the "Flying Novena" by the devout in New Orleans. It's kind of a drive-through worship for those in a hurry.

Our Lady of Guadalupe is also a shrine to St. Jude, the patron saint of hopeless causes. You can take your hopeless cause prayer to the sanctuary's right then go to the left side of the sanctuary to ask St. Expedite to, well, expedite it.

The Voodoo connection makes St. Expedite a versatile spiritual player. Today, believers surreptitiously leave offerings of colored candles, water, flowers and rum along with the preferred offering of pound cake usually left at the tomb of Marie Laveau. For those interested, the go-to pound cake is said to be Sara Lee.

Some may be put off by the pagan aspects of St. Expedite, but it is pointed out that only positive requests are honored.

EX-J&M RECORDING STUDIO

The birthplace of rock'n'roll?

840 North Rampart
Tel: 504-522-1336
Open: Mon–Sat 8am–7pm, Sunday 8am–4pm
#91 Jackson/Esplanade bus, #57 Franklin Avenue bus or#88 St Claude/Jackson
Barracks, Rampart/St Claude Streetcar

On the edge of the French Quarter, the laundromat at 840 North Rampart is a landmark of American culture; this was the site of Cosimo Matassa's J&M Recording Studio, the birthplace of rock'n'roll. At the entrance, a terrazzo sign says simply 'J&M Music Shop'. Two historical plaques flank the doorway of the laundromat to mark the significance of this cultural real estate. It was here on December 10, 1949, that Fats Domino recorded his song 'The Fat Man', which some historians consider the first rock'n'roll song. For those who doubt the historical importance, Matassa also recorded Little Richard's 'Tutti Frutti' and Roy Brown's 'Good Rockin' Tonite' - all three are contenders for the honors of the first rock'n'roll record.

If there is no definitive place or record that can be agreed upon as the spot or song that gave birth to rock'n'roll, this building has as much claim to the distinction as any other in the world. It was exactly here that Matassa, in a small room in the rear of his father's store, helped to create the genres of rock'n'roll and rhythm and blues by recording the likes of Fats Domino, Little Richard, Dave Bartholomew, Sam Cooke and Professor Longhair, to name only a few of the icons of American pop music who created magic between 1945 and 1955. In fact, almost every rhythm and blues song recorded in New Orleans from the late 40s to the early 70s was recorded by Matassa. Even the room itself was considered an instrument. Matassa, who was inducted into the Rock'n'Roll Hall of Fame in 2012 as a non-performer, is given credit with creating what came to be called 'the Cosimo sound' (or 'New Orleans sound'), which consisted of strong drums, heavy guitar, bass, heavy piano, light horn and a strong vocal lead.

The list of musical talent that Matassa nurtured and facilitated at his studio is mind-blowing. Besides Domino and Richards, young guns like Allen Toussaint and Dr. John got their starts here; even early rock icon Jerry Lee Lewis came down from Ferriday, LA. to make his first demo tape at Cosimo's. All presumably soaking up the music from the likes of Dave Bartholomew (who produced many of the hits), Ray Charles, Lloyd Price, Smiley Lewis, Irma Thomas, Sam Cooke, Guitar Slim and drummer Earl Palmer, who is given credit for introducing the backbeat at a J&M session (an innovation that supplies the bedrock of rock'n'roll drumming).

The studio at 840 N. Rampart was designated a Historical Significant Landmark of Rock'n'Roll by the Rock Hall of Fame in 2010. It is one of 11 such designations around the country.

Matassa moved to a larger studio at 525 Governor Nicholls in 1955 and eventually moved his operations to 748 Camp, the present site of Rebellion Restaurant, which has bronze records in concrete to commemorate the last hits Matassa recorded at his studio on Camp street, such as Lee Dorsey's, 'Working in a Coal Mine' and Ivan Neville's 'Tell It Like It is'.

JOHN L. SULLIVAN'S ARM CAST ⑥

*The last bare knuckles heavyweight champion
of the world*

New Orleans Athletic Club
222 N. Rampart Street
Tel: 504-525-2375 - www.neworleansathleticclub.com
Open: Every day 5:30pm–9pm
*Rampart-St. Claude streetcar or Canal streetcar or #88 St. Claude/Jackson
Barracks bus*

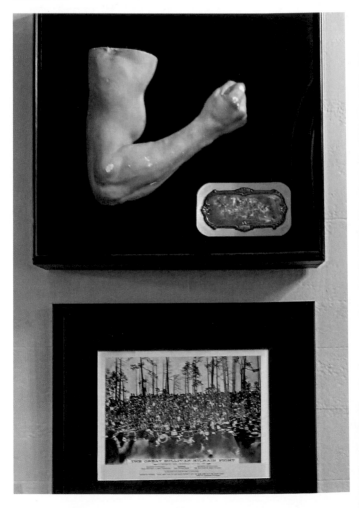

Situated on the northern edge of the French Quarter on N. Rampart, the New Orleans Athletic Club opened in 1872 and has long served as a place for athletic activity such as swimming, running and weight lifting. It has also served as a social fixture in the city's history. Businessmen would meet at the 'club' to share camaraderie, play gin rummy and schmooze.

Just a few feet inside the front door, a case on the wall behind the receptionist desk speaks of the athletic legacy. It contains a plaster cast of the right arm of John L. Sullivan, the last bare knuckles heavyweight champion of the world and a patron of the club. Sullivan trained at the NOAC before his historic last fight in 1889 and the cast itself was made in New Orleans.

The case also displays a tarnished championship boxing belt. Below the case is a rare photo of the bout featuring Sullivan and his opponent Jake Kilrain in a clinch as a throng of spectators look on expectantly.

The bout itself was held in Richburg, Mississippi, as bare knuckles boxing had been outlawed in over 38 states, including Louisiana and Mississippi. The authorities tried to stop the fight with troops reportedly stationed along the way to prevent the breaking of the law. Consequently, the fighters, promoters and spectators had to proceed in what was described as "stealth" to the Mississippi site.

Sullivan was one of the most famous men in America and widespread speculation had him ripe for the picking after two recent bouts, in one of which he broke an arm and another that ended in a draw. Kilrain, a huge challenger, had fought the champion of England to a draw and it was believed that the aging Sullivan could not withstand a long bout as he had never gone longer than nine rounds in any of his previous fights.

The fight lasted 75 rounds. A round in those days ended when one or both of the fighters went down, either by punch or in a clinch. The July day was cloudless and hot and the bout turned out to be the toughest of Sullivan's career. Yet after the 75th round, Kilrain's handlers asked for a draw. Sullivan turned them down, so they threw in the sponges and Sullivan retained his championship.

IRISH CULTURAL MUSEUM OF NEW ORLEANS

One of the underappreciated ethnic communities of New Orleans

933 Conti Street
Tel: 504-481-8139
www.icmnola.com
Open: Mon–Thurs 8am–4pm, Fri–Sat 8am–7:30 pm, closed Sunday
Free entry
Rampart-St. Claude streetcar

Marching sashes worn by New Orleans Ancient Order of Hibernian member William Mahon circa 1902 (donated to the Ancient Order of Hibernians of Louisiana by grandniece, Wetsa Mattie Stigner via Cathleen Calder)

One of the newest (and surely one of the smallest) museums in New Orleans Is the Irish Cultural Museum, opened in 2015 in the French Quarter in a beautifully restored Spanish colonial building that survived both of New Orleans' catastrophic fires in 1788 and 1794. It is dedicated to informing the public about one of the most underappreciated ethnic communities of New Orleans. When the outside world thinks of New Orleans, they usually think of French, Spanish or African heritage. This museum was established to familiarize visitors to the city with the unique, important and all-encompassing contributions from its Irish citizenry that made New Orleans what it was and is today.

The exhibits are housed in one small room entered from the courtyard. They include photos, texts, and very few artifacts; the bulk of the information is provided by video screens, one of which tells of the Irish Potato Famine (1845-1852) and its enormous impact on immigration to the United States.

New Orleans was one of the main recipients of that immigration. As the second largest port in the United States in the 1840s, the city already had a significant Irish community. For example, the second Governor of Louisiana, Alexander O'Reilly, was an Irishman. New Orleans, at the bottom of the Mississippi River Valley, also provided a perfect jumping off point for those wishing to get to the American heartland.

By 1860, one in five citizens of New Orleans was of Irish descent and the city's history is replete with successful Irish Americans in every imaginable field of endeavor. Many everyday citizens contributed to New Orleans' success; you need go no further than the digging of the New Basin Canal that is prominently covered in the Irish Museum. Thousands of laborers died while digging this important economic engine of the city; most were Irish.

Three Irish Americans of note highlighted on an interactive touchscreen video include; John McDonogh, who at his death gave his entire fortune to establish dozens of public schools for both black and white children in New Orleans and Baltimore; Margaret Haughery, an orphan who established a successful bakery and gave untold amounts of money to the poor; and one of the most unsung of U.S. revolutionary patriots, Oliver Pollock, the New Orleans financier, who gave almost all of his vast fortune to finance the American Revolution. In fact, Pollock was the single highest contributor to the cause for independence; he died penniless because of his financial commitment.

Pollock has another distinction known only to the most serious history buffs: it is he who is given credit for popularizing the U.S. dollar sign, which he used in his financial dealings and is thought to be derived from a symbol for the Spanish dollar.

GERMAINE WELLS MARDI GRAS MUSEUM

A queen of over 17 Mardi Gras krewes from 1937 to 1968

813 Bienville Street
Tel: 504-523-5433
Open: Every day from 6pm until the restaurant's closing time
Rampart-St. Claude streetcar or Canal streetcar

O n the second floor of Arnaud's, one of New Orleans' great old Creole restaurants, the Germaine Cazenave Wells Mardi Gras Museum is dedicated to Ms. Wells and her colorful life and passion for Mardi Gras. Wells was the daughter of Count Arnaud Cazenave, the founder of Arnaud's.

Wells reigned as queen from 1937 to 1968 for over 17 different carnival organizations, 22 times more than any other woman in New Orleans Mardi Gras history.

The museum, which is open to the public free of charge seven days a week whenever the restaurant is open for business, consists of dozens of vintage photos of Wells' social life, Mardi Gras jewelry, krewe favors and children's Mardi Gras costumes. But pride of place goes to over a dozen gowns she wore as queen.

The gowns, displayed in glass cases, range in a variety of styles from Middle Eastern potentate to a champagne themed design adorned with large yellowish grapes to a simple yet exquisite fairy princess. All are very reminiscent of wedding dresses and come complete with dramatic trains displayed here fanned out against the back walls of the exhibits extended like large caped wings.

The first glass case you encounter when visiting the museum does not pertain to Mardi Gras but to another lasting contribution Ms. Wells made to New Orleans social milieu. It contains a display of several of Wells' substantially large Easter bonnets.

Her evident love for the spectacle of parades was not satiated by her Mardi Gras honors. In 1956 she started an Easter parade in the French Quarter that would proceed in mule-drawn carriages from Arnaud's to St. Louis Cathedral for mass then back to Arnaud's.

Her spring parade was inspired by the Easter parade in New York City and quickly became a New Orleans tradition. Ms. Wells passed away in 1983, yet her parade lives on.

BEVOLO WORKSHOP & MUSEUM

The romantic atmospherics of the Quarter

Bevolo workshop & museum
318 Royal Street
Tel: 504-552-4311
www.bevolo.com
Open: Every day 9am–4:30pm
Canal streetcar, Riverfront streetcar and #5 Marigny-Bywater bus

O n Exchange Place, an open doorway leads into the back of a shop on Royal Street in the French Quarter. Simply walk in to find a workshop where you will see craftsman at work on the trademark French Quarter Lamp.

The story begins in 1945 when Anthony Bevolo, Jr. opened his shop. Bevolo put into action techniques he had learned over his career while working most notably for Ford, Igor Sikorsky and Andrew Higgins. His revolutionary idea was to build gas light frames by riveting the metalwork as opposed to the older, more common process of soldering, thereby creating a more durable and stronger product.

Enter the other player in the creation of the French Quarter Lamp that is now ubiquitous in the Vieux Carré. A. Hays Town (1903-2005), a young architect facilitated by the open workshop, simply walked in off the street and asked Bevolo if he could make a certain kind of gas lamp from a design of his own. Bevolo told Town that if he could draw it for him he could make it.

Today, the dozens and dozens of lamps contribute greatly to the romantic atmospherics of the Quarter and provide one of the go-to images artists choose to evoke the ambience of the Quarter in everything from advertisements to book covers and movie posters. The style can be seen almost literally on every block of the Quarter.

The workshop itself appears unchanged from the one Town ambled into on that fateful day when he and Bevolo first met. You can watch and speak to the craftsmen as they fashion the familiar design. The lamps are all fabricated by hand using antiqued copper, serving a worldwide client list with over 500 design variations.

Hays Town became a distinguished architect, first recognized for his modernist designs and later in life for his residential work, which relied heavily on Spanish, French and Creole Louisiana history. Many of his designs are so distinctive that they bear plaques heralding them as 'A. Hays Town designed'.

The timeline on the wall provides a history lesson on gas and electric public lighting, picking up in 1945 with the story of the Bevolo company.

This small workshop and museum is indeed a surprise to most who come across it, including many lifelong residents of the city.

GROUCHO'S BERET

An ad hoc museum

Antoine's restaurant
713 St. Louis
Tel: 504-581-4422 - www.antoines.com
Open: Every day 11:30am–2pm and 5:30pm–9pm
Riverfront streetcar or #5 Marigny-Bywater bus

Antoine's, the oldest restaurant in the United States still under the control of the family that founded it, is truly a museum unto itself. Among the many artifacts, Groucho Marx's beret (the one he wore on his first European tour) is displayed in a glass case surrounded by ashtrays, dinnerware, glasses, bottles, and other bric-à-brac. The simple hat, worn by one of the most iconic figures of world cinema and an important figure in American cultural life, may be one of the best-kept secrets in the city. A gift to Antoine's proprietor Roy Alciatore, the dark blue beret is accompanied by a letter from Groucho himself.

Once you get past the traditional main dining room and its old world charm, numerous other dining rooms teem with memorabilia and history. Photos of the famous who have dined there are framed on the walls; Jean Harlow, J. Edgar Hoover and George Patton in one seven-foot square section of wall alone. There are many others throughout the restaurant, including a signed photo of the three Marx Brothers.

The 'collection' is a grab bag of cool: glassware from the House of Napoleon, glassware and dinnerware from potentates around the world, an original Edison light bulb, a rare silver duck press (you may bring your own duck), and countless other items can be found here.

Each dining room has its own personality. The Rex Room, for example, is where the King of Carnival and his party have a pre-parade meal surrounded by Mardi Gras memorabilia such as costumes, jewelry and ball favors.

Then there is the Proteus Room, the Snail Room, the Japanese Room (closed after Pearl Harbor and not reopened until 1999) and, of course, the Mystery Room. Next to the main dining room, the Mystery Room came by its name during prohibition. The story goes that during that time, ladies would excuse themselves, enter the adjacent room through the rest room and return with coffee cups filled with liquor. When asked, "Where did you get the beverage?" the ladies would answer simply, "It's a mystery."

The origin of the word 'appetizer'

In a large frame in the second dining room, hanging beside photos of celebrities, is the story of how the word 'appetizer' was coined. In the early 1950s, the United States Restaurant Association wanted to replace the word hors d'oeuvre, which it considered too European, with a more American appellation. Roy Alciatore, the proprietor of Antoine's at the time, submitted the winning entry, "Appetite Teaser", which became the word 'appetizer' we use today.

M.S. RAU ANTIQUES' SECRET ROOM ⑪

An eclectic catalog of goods only hinted at by the storefront

630 Royal Street
Tel: 1-888-711-8084 or 855-640-8046
Email: info@rauantiques.com
Open: Mon–Sat 9am–5:15pm
#5 Marigny-Bywater bus or Riverfront streetcar

M.S. Rau Antiques - North America's largest antique emporium - is well known for its luxurious French Quarter showroom, beautiful antiques and jewelry from Cartier, Tiffany and Van Cleef & Arpels. Its "secret room," is much less famous, though it can be accessed by simply asking for it politely.

A secret trompe l'oeil door opens into a tastefully lit corridor with a row of pedestals displaying exquisite and expensive works of art, such as Napoleon's death mask. Over three floors, the secret room houses an array of museum quality treasures, many with great historical as well as artistic value.

On any given day you may find here original paintings by the likes of Monet, Norman Rockwell, Toulouse Lautrec, de Kooning, Hassam, Chagall and Van Gogh, just to drop a few names.

Other interesting artifacts that are on hand or have previously been for sale are mint quality vintage arcade games, a player piano in a gorgeous wood armoire with player violins, a World War II Enigma machine, a 150,000-year-old Ice Age bear skeleton standing eight feet tall, and even an intricate seven-piece bedroom set from the bedroom of King Farouk. All of these have at one time been among the eclectic catalog of goods only hinted at by the small, ornate storefront on Royal Street. And the collection is always changing because, unlike in a museum, everything you see here is for sale.

The sex chair of Queen Victoria's son, Prince Edward

The most provocative and talked about item ever sold at M.S. Rau was a sex chair built in the 1880s for Queen Victoria's son, Prince Edward. It was designed to hold his weight during forays to French bordellos in the days before he became King Edward VII.

ST. ANTHONY'S GARDEN

A towering shadow of Jesus

615 Pere Antoine Alley
Tel: 504-525-9585
www.cathedral@arch-no.org
Cathedral open daily 8:30am–4pm
Garden closed to the public
Riverfront streetcar and #5 Marigny-Bywater bus

I f you are walking along Bourbon Street at night, take a look down Orleans Avenue toward the river. You will see that the tranquil park behind St. Louis Cathedral has been transformed into a striking tableau somehow at odds with the prevalent libertine image of the French Quarter. A spotlight trained on the towering statue of the Sacred Heart of Jesus (arms outstretched, palms open) projects a dramatic shadow against the back wall of the Cathedral.

Here is St. Anthony's Garden. It sits in near anonymity behind the most enduring landmark in the skyline of New Orleans' French Quarter, the St. Louis Cathedral, the oldest active cathedral in the United States. Behind a wrought-iron fence partially cloaked in hedges and vines (as well as the daily wares of artists who have hawked their work here for almost a century), the garden is awash in the history of the Crescent City, yet goes all but unnoticed among the urban hubbub of daytime hours.

St. Anthony's Garden rests in the heart of the Quarter; a silent sentinel of history flanked by more recent manifestations of the city's culture. On one side of the garden fence, Pirate's Alley is home to number 624, where William Faulkner wrote his first novel *Soldiers Pay*. On the other side the alley at the corner of Pere Antoine and Royal sits the gallery of the late George Rodrigue, famous for his 'Blue Dog' paintings of the 1990s.

The garden actually predates the famous church and has served many different purposes over the years. It has been a vegetable garden, a public market place from 1830 to 1860, and a sanctuary. There have even been some dubious claims that it was once a site of duels. Since 1890, St. Anthony's Garden has been a private space.

The garden is named after St. Anthony of Lisbon and Padua, 'finder of lost things'. However, it is closely identified with his namesake, a Spanish Capuchin friar named Antonio de Sedella or 'Père Antoine', who came to be an almost legendary New Orleans figure. Père Antoine's ghost is said to walk the alleyway named after him.

The garden is also the scene of social events for local charities, drawing movie stars and literary celebrities. One event included the spectacle of famed Beat Generation poet Lawrence Ferlinghetti crashing a soiree while bedecked in an animal mask.

During Hurricane Katrina, a large oak tree in the garden was blown down, damaging the Sacred Heart of Jesus statue. Archbishop Emeritus Alfred Hughes vowed not to repair the statue until after the city had recovered from the storm. True to his word, the Archbishop did not allow its restoration until 2010.

NEW ORLEANS PHARMACY MUSEUM

The very first pharmacist ever licensed by the United States government

514 Chartres Street
Tel: 504-565-8027 - www.pharmacymuseum.org
Open: Tue–Sat 10am–4pm
Entry fee: Adults $5, Students & Seniors $4, Children under six free
Riverfront streetcar and #5 Marigny-Bywater bus

In the heart of the French Quarter, a mortar and pestle sign reads, "La Pharmacie Francaise." The sign marks the spot of the New Orleans Pharmacy Museum, a gem of a small museum housed in a building built

in 1823 by Louis Dulfiho Jr., the very first pharmacist ever licensed by the United States government. The windows are filled with show globes - large glass containers filled with colored water. As early as the 14th century, these globes identified shops where medicine was available. The ground floor of the museum is packed with informative displays of a wide variety of vintage medicinal items. Most of the labeled apothecary jars hold plant, animal and mineral materials with exotic names such as red serpent, pythritrum, gum oliban and quilluja - all substances used by pharmacists to make the medicines of the time. Items in the two-storey museum cover the gamut of disciplines and materials familiar to the pharmacist of yesteryear. There are exhibits on dentistry, alcohol use, bitters, patent medicines, surgery, eyewear, homeopathic medicine, midwifery and even a case of voodoo remedies and potions. It seems in New Orleans it was understood that you could go to the drug store to purchase voodoo items, although they were generally to be kept under the counter. You'll see an example of these offbeat items on a shelf inside one of dozens of hand carved mahogany fixtures from Germany.

Louis Dulfiho Jr. was born in France but the family moved to New Orleans in the early 19th century. Dulfiho Jr. later studied and graduated from the College of Pharmacy in Paris and moved back to New Orleans. He opened a pharmacy at 63 Chartres Street with his brother, before eventually opening his own pharmacy at 514 Chartres, the site of today's museum.

French and Spanish administrations had standards for pharmacists before the time of the Louisiana Purchase in 1803, but in America an informal apprenticeship led to the profession. However, the first American governor of Louisiana, William Claiborne, had a law passed requiring pharmacists practicing in Louisiana to pass a test. The requirement was a three-hour oral exam that Louis Dulfhio Jr. was the first to complete successfully.

There is courtyard at the rear of the property and it is thought the pharmacists of that bygone day used the garden to grow the herbs and plants utilized in making medicines.

An old-fashioned, still functional soda fountain

To the right of the front entrance of the building is an old-fashioned soda fountain, claimed to be still functional. Although materials used to build the inner workings make it unusable, the beauty of the 1855 Italian black and rose marble specimen gives a flavor of how it looked back in the day.

MARBLE HALL

The finest business hall in the world

423 Canal Street
Tel: 504-589-6094 ext 111 (call ahead to make arrangements)
www.gsa.gov/portal/ext/html/site/hb/category/25431/actionParameter/
exploreByBuilding/buildingId/925
Open: Mon–Fri 8am–5pm
Canal streetcar

A magnificent public space now hidden from view inside a federal build-ing on the second floor, the Marble Hall is perhaps the most beautiful interior in New Orleans.

Called the finest Greek Revival interior in the United States, in its heyday it was considered the finest business hall in the world. Today it sits mostly silent, used only sparingly for special occasions. It is a revelation when first seen, but is relatively unknown even among lifelong Orlean-ians. It stands 55 feet high, 128 feet long and 54 feet wide, its cornice supported by 14 huge 41-foot Corinthian columns, each topped with the heads of Mercury, god of commerce (among other duties), and Luna, whose crescent shaped brows are a nod to the crescent shape of the city.

The ceiling is a geometric pattern of glass that allows natural sunlight to enter the chamber. Hand cranks that were once used to open the

roof for ventilation in the days before air conditioning are still present. On the N. Peters Street entrance, now the side entrance, are large bas-relief sculptures of Bienville (the founder of New Orleans), Andrew Jackson (the hero of the Battle of New Orleans), and a pelican feeding her young, the symbol of the State of Louisiana.

Construction began in 1848 with a cornerstone laid by the great American statesman Henry Clay, but the building was not finished until eight architects later, after the intervention of the Civil War in 1881. Ship's captains would declare their cargo and pay their tariffs in this great room, the floor of which lay over a large carriageway to transfer that cargo. The room was used for this purpose right up until Hurricane Katrina in 2005. Renovated in 1961 and again in 1993, the building now houses various federal offices. As of 2008, part of the building has been home to Audubon Butterfly Garden and Insectarium, the largest free standing insect museum in the United States. Take a close look at the front exterior of the massive U.S. Customhouse near the foot of Canal Street and you'll see large modified Egyptian Revival columns. You'll probably be struck by the size of the building that occupies a whole square city block. In fact, when work to build the structure commenced in 1848 it was to be the second largest building in the United States behind the United States Capitol. Not everyone was impressed, though; Mark Twain remarked that it reminded him of a large icebox.

NIMS JAZZ WALK OF FAME

Once known as a hotbed of Voodoo and Hoodoo

De Armas Street at Algiers Point
Open: 6.45am–11.45pm
www.nps.gov/jazz
Algiers Ferry or #101 Algiers bus

At the top of the Mississippi River levee at Algiers Point, to the right after you disembark the Algiers Ferry from the east bank, stands a statue of Louis Armstrong. The statue marks the Robert E. Nims Jazz Walk of Fame, administered by the National Park Service. The walk affords a distinctive view of the French Quarter on one side of the river and on the other, a glimpse of Algiers, the second oldest neighborhood in the city.

The Jazz Walk provides a roster of New Orleans musical greats celebrated by old-fashioned streetlights adorned with likenesses and biographies of many of the musicians who brought the music to the world. It is appropriately positioned to look down onto the West Bank community where an enormous array of the earliest practitioners of this New Orleans-bred music genre lived and played.

Those honored include Armstrong, Buddy Bolden, Kid Ory, Jelly Roll Morton, Pete Fountain, Al Hirt, Nick LaRocca and Louis Prima. The list reminds us of the ethnic diversity represented in the jazz pantheon of New Orleans.

Algiers, which was called the "Brooklyn of the South" and was known all over the country in African-American communities as a hot bed of Voodoo and Hoodoo, boasted 36 music venues at one time in the early 20th century. Many jazz musicians called this area home. Notable among those "Algerians" (as the residents were known) were Henry "Red" Allen, George Lewis, Elizabeth "Memphis Minnie" Douglas, "Kid Thomas" Valentine, Papa Celestin and many prominent musical families such as the Adams, Brunis, Dast, Manetta and Marcour families to name but a few.

The National Park Service offers an audio tour at its French Quarter station and many of the homes still standing are only a short walk away from the river. There is also a self-guided tour available online provided by the Algiers Historical Society.

WILLIAMS BURROUGHS' HOUSE

Home of a legendary experimental American writer

509 Wagner Street, Algiers
Private residence not open to the public
#101 Algiers Loop bus

The quiet middle class homes in the Algiers section of New Orleans may seem like an unusual place to find a plaque dedicated to a legendary experimental American writer. But here it is, at 509 Wagner Street, the home of William S. Burroughs, from 1948 to 1949.

The house that today seems relatively innocuous, behind a chain link fence with a palmetto tree in front, was described as a "dilapidated sagging heap with an interesting porch" by Jack Kerouac in his book *On The Road*.

"It was a wonderful porch. It ran clear around the house," Kerouac wrote.

Well, it only goes halfway around the house now. And the sagging wooden porch is now a renovated concrete version of its former self.

Burroughs said he chose to move his family into this suburban environment, as opposed to the more bohemian landscape of New Orleans, simply because it was the cheapest neighborhood in which to live.

Burroughs lived here with his common law wife Joan Vollmer and their two children. They were visited during their brief stay in the city by Beat luminaries such as Kerouac and Allen Ginsberg, but left after being arrested by New Orleans police for drug possession and firearm violations, escaping the law by moving to Mexico.

While in Mexico, Burroughs shot and killed Ms. Vollmer in a drunken re-enactment of the William Tell legend, an incident to which he credited the impetus of his writing career.

Best known for the controversial novel *Naked Lunch*, Burroughs went on to become one of the most culturally significant and innovative artists of the 20th century. His importance to popular culture is attested to by the range of musicians who were influenced by his creative force. The list includes Frank Zappa, Patti Smith, Tom Waits, Philip Glass, U2, Kurt Cobain, John Cage and The Beatles. He was (and still is) so iconic that he is one of the notable figures featured on the cover of The Beatles' classic album *Sgt. Pepper's Lonely Heart Club Band*.

In 1996, a plaque was placed in front of the house to mark Burroughs' short sojourn in New Orleans. The marker was sponsored by the Eisenhower Center for American Studies at the University of New Orleans.

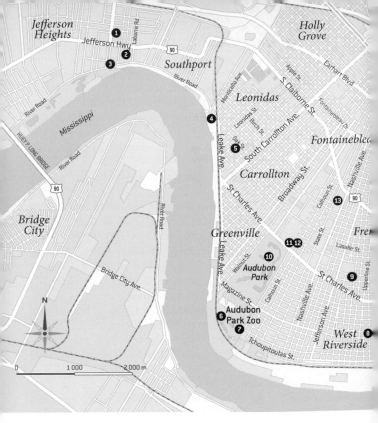

Uptown

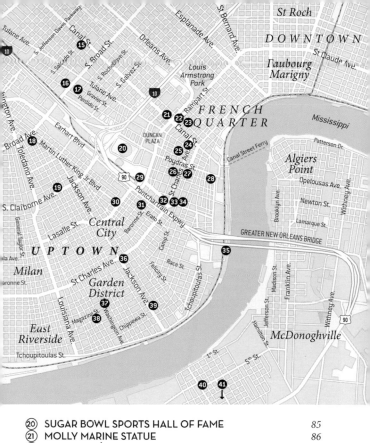

SOUTHERN PACIFIC T-NO 745 LOCOMOTIVE

Only one of 12 remaining in operating condition

1501 Jefferson Highway
Tel: 504-539-4600
Email: web@lasta.org
Open: Saturday 8am–2pm
#E3 Kenner Loop bus

The Southern Pacific T-NO 745, a refurbished Mikado type 2-8-2 steam locomotive, bides its time in an almost secret location behind the parking lot of the sprawling Ochsner Medical Center, which surrounds a vintage railroad car graveyard.

The locomotive sits in a railroad yard behind the parking lot off Jefferson Highway like a racehorse hidden away in its stable primed and ready to run at a moment's notice.

Fourteen thousand locomotives of this type were built in North America during the heyday of rail travel. Today, the Southern Pacific 745 is one of only 12 remaining in operating condition. The Mikado type engine is indeed a thoroughbred, a classic among locomotives and considered the classic American freight locomotive from what is called the golden era of steam before the railroad industry converted to diesel and electric technology.

The railroad baron E. H. Harriman insisted that all his locomotives be built to a standard design based on the best features known at the time. Indeed, designs identical or similar to the 2-8-2 type locomotive were used all over the world.

Built at a railroad yard in Algiers during World War I, the 745 was completed in 1921 and restored by the Louisiana Railway Heritage Trust after it was moved to its present site from Audubon Park in 1984. The trust is a non-profit volunteer group whose stated mission is to educate and entertain the public about railroading, particularly steam powered rail.

The 745 is the only surviving locomotive built in Louisiana.

The '2-8-2' refers to the wheel arrangement; this design allowed for specific placement of the firebox to generate greater horsepower, allowing this model to reach higher speeds.

The 745 was placed on the U.S. National Register of Historic Places and in 2007 took its first trip since its retirement from regular service in 1956. It is now used for occasional excursions in the Louisiana and Mississippi areas and has traveled as far as Kansas City.

OCHSNER DIMES

Thirty pieces of silver

Ochsner Clinic
1514 Jefferson Highway
Tel: 866-624-7637
www.ochsner.org
E-3 Kenner Local bus

As you enter the hospital wing of Ochsner Clinic, the corridor is lined by a series of glass cases displaying large museum-like text. The text tells the story of this great medical institution, started in 1942 by Dr. Alton Ochsner and four colleagues, which grew into the internationally known medical facility it is today.

The Joseph Rault timeline has one very interesting artifact: a small leather bag with its former contents fanned out in front of it. Thirty silver dimes, or, if you will, 30 pieces of silver.

In the late 30s and early 40s, Dr. Ochsner and four physicians started a group practice that would ultimately be named Ochsner Clinic. At that time, the group practice concept was found nowhere in the southern United States and was considered by the local medical community in New Orleans to be a threat to the prevailing medical business plan. All doctors in New Orleans were sole practitioners and this novel business approach was viewed with deep suspicion.

On the morning of Holy Thursday, 1941, Ochsner and the four other members of his group practice woke up to find leather bags each containing 30 dimes. The implication was clear: the doctors involved in the clinic were seen as traitors (or Judases) to their colleagues. The incident was so fraught with emotion, the gesture so jarring, that it is said that the animosity between the Ochsner group and the local medical community lingered for decades.

Today, this event is all but forgotten. Ochsner Clinic is a household word in Greater New Orleans and renowned all over the country.

Dr. Alton Ochsner, who was descended from a long line of physicians going back to 15th-century Switzerland, came to New Orleans to head the Department of Surgery at Tulane University in 1927 at the age of 31. He became a physician of note after writing a groundbreaking article for a prominent medical journal. He was one of the first to link lung cancer and cigarette smoking, a claim he stuck to doggedly despite receiving much ridicule for his position.

In his position at Tulane University, Dr. Ochsner is given credit for organizing one of America's premier surgical teaching hospitals at New Orleans Charity Hospital.

He was an accomplished surgeon, performing the first successful separation of conjoined twins in which both twins survived. He performed over 20,000 surgeries in his career, even performing operations up until his final day of work at 70 years of age.

CAMP PARAPET

The only site left over from the Civil War

Half a block east of the intersection of Causeway Blvd. and Arlington Street
www.jeffersonhistoricalsociety.com
Open: one Saturday a year in the fall – on Camp Parapet Day
E-5 Causeway bus or E-3 Kenner Local bus

Swallowed up by an aging suburbia just about two football fields away as the crow flies from the Mississippi River in Jefferson Parish (near American Legion Hall 267), Camp Parapet is the only site in the greater New Orleans area left over from the Civil War.

Behind padlocked gates and a chain link fence, the powder magazine - the single remaining building of the once extensive military complex - can easily be seen from the street. In 1984, the powder magazine and the immediate surroundings were restored and now serve as a historical reminder of the war for school children and visitors on tours arranged through the Jefferson Historical Society.

Camp Parapet was designed to protect the city from a Union invasion. The fort was originally named Fort John Hunt Morgan after a Kentucky war hero. The Union invasion, however, came from the south when Admiral David Farragut's fleet took the city and the Confederate forces in a panic tried to sabotage the fort. The fortifications fell into the hands of the Union forces and the site was named Camp Parapet. The Union forces garrisoned Camp Parapet for the rest of the war to fend off a Confederate invasion that never came.

The camp once boasted a hot shot furnace, an observatory, a guard house, officers' quarters and nine heavy artillery guns. Now all that remains is a brick enclosed structure in an earthen mound that served as a powder magazine.

Even though it experienced no fighting during the war, the fort can still claim some important historical significance. After the Union took possession of the fortification, freed slaves flocked to the fort in search of food and shelter often with families in tow. Many who came were given jobs as laborers or assistants and many ended up serving under General John Walcott, a strict abolitionist from Vermont.

The 73rd Regiment United States Colored Troops that served at Camp Parapet during the war were the first African American regiment formed in the Union Army. The 73rd regiment famously fought with valor during the Port Hudson campaign. The African American forces at Port Hudson were also the first African American troops who would serve under African American field leadership. One of those officers, P.B.S. Pinchback, later became the first African American to serve as governor of a U.S. state, an event that wouldn't occur again until 1990.

Due to poor hygienic conditions, deaths were so prevalent at the site that it served as a cemetery for 7,000 soldiers who were later moved to Chalmette National Cemetery. The camp has continued to serve as a cemetery for two area church congregations. The facilities left over from the war also served as the Jefferson Parish lockup until the 1920s.

BATTURE HOUSES

Enclave of houses on stilts

Intersection of Dakin Street and Monticello Avenue right off River Road
St. Charles streetcar

Just outside the city limits on the banks of the Mississippi River, there is an enclave of houses on stilts near the New Orleans/Jefferson Parish line. The row of about a dozen houses hovering over the river is known as 'the Batture' and is one of New Orleans' most interesting neighborhoods.

The architectural style of the homes varies; they seem to be a mixture of do-it-yourself and more modern building techniques. Most have walkways leading to small galleries that surround the houses, allowing access to the shore when the river rises at flood time each year.

At one time, houses such as these were the norm on the city's waterfront. But now, only these few remain.

Ownership of the land presents an interesting puzzle; by precedent of law, the lots are considered part of the river rather than the city. As such, the homes are afforded neither garbage collection nor a hydrant for firefighting.

Just who owns the land is in dispute. It is claimed that the ownership of the property is grandfathered in due to the legal concept of squatter's rights. However, a local attorney who hails from a family that ran and owned the popular gambling hall just yards across River Road has claimed ownership. So far the courts have disagreed with this claim.

The historical nature of the camps on the Batture is attested to by a court case that goes all the way back to 1810, when President Thomas Jefferson won the case against the esteemed New Orleans attorney Robert Livingston, establishing the ownership of the Batture for the federal government.

A touch of urban poetry was perhaps involved in the naming of the street that leads up the levee from River Road across the levee to the Batture. It serves as the mailing address for the Batture residents: Monticello Street.

EVERETTE MADDOX POETRY READING

⑤

Oldest continuous poetry reading in the South

Maple Leaf Bar
8316 Oak Street
Tel: 504-866-9359
www.mapleleafbar.com
Open: Readings are on Sundays at 3pm (more or less)
St. Charles streetcar

O n Sundays at 3pm, among the worn bricks, assorted metal chairs, tables and exotic subtropical plants that grace the patio at the back of the Maple Leaf Bar, you will find the Everette Maddox Memorial Reading series. This tradition, started by the late poet Everette Maddox, has lasted for over 30 years, making it the oldest continuing poetry reading in the South, if not the nation.

The reading is lovingly run by Everette's friend and fellow poet Nancy Harris. Poets and poetry fans gather to listen to published poets, ne'er-do-well poets, famous poets, almost famous poets, and should-be-famous poets in the patio of the bar, which is more widely known for its music of local favorites. Luminaries such as the late James Booker, Walter "Wolfman" Washington, Rockin' Dopsie and the Rebirth Brass Band are among the many acts that have performed in the bar. Beyoncé once used the bar as a backdrop for a promotional video and it's not unusual for internationally known musicians such as Bonnie Raitt or Bruce Springsteen to drop by and sit in with a local group.

But on Sundays poetry has the spotlight. You can catch the varied voices of the Crescent City's muse, often accompanied by banter about the beloved poet who started it all, Everette Maddox, who is at rest just a few feet away.

Everette Maddox – He was a mess

Born in Alabama, Everette Maddox moved to New Orleans from Alabama to take a teaching position at a local university. He died here in 1989. His poems appeared in such publications as the New Yorker and Paris Review, and he is remembered by the burial of his ashes in the patio marked by a plaque that reads, "Everette Maddox - He was a mess."

Maddox spent his last years as the resident poet at the bar. He would often write his latest works on napkins and coasters, which his friends collected. With the help of the bar's owner, Hank Staples, they would be published in the posthumous collection *American Waste*.

For the last word - although thanks to Everette and friends, there really is no last word - we'll defer to Julie Kane, former Poet Laureate of Louisiana and one of the most prominent alumni of the reading:

"Everette Maddox was like a human supernova, flaring brilliantly just before extinction in the Maple Leaf Bar. He was an intellectual genius, a gifted poet, a standup comic, a loyal friend. And he was one of the most charismatic individuals I have ever encountered. His life ended too soon, but his legend will never die."

WPA BRICK BAS RELIEFS - AUDUBON ZOO

Beautiful and under recognized artwork by WPA

6500 Magazine Street
Tel: 504-861-2537
www.audubonnatureinstitute.org/zoo
Open: Mon–Fri 10am–5pm, Sat–Sun 10am–6pm
#11 Magazine bus

T he fine bas-reliefs still visible on older brick structures at Audubon Zoo are some of the more beautiful and under recognized artwork created by the Works Progress Administration (WPA) in New Orleans.

Soon after entering the zoo, you may or may not notice the reliefs of birds in flight on the original birdhouse, a brick building to the left where whooping cranes reside. The brick relief work was created in the 1930s and is camouflaged to blend in with the background. The relief continues around the side of the building, with other animal figures obscured behind foliage above the foraging cranes.

Further into the zoo, past the Elephant Fountain, you'll find the largest and finest brick reliefs on towers flanking the entrance to a new water play area for children. The legendary tortoise and hare are on one side, with a wolf howling at an invisible moon on the other.

Audubon Zoo, one of the finest zoological parks in the nation, was substantially constructed by the WPA. The zoo was updated in the 1970s and 1980s, transforming it into the modern park it is now.

Audubon Park itself occupies land that constituted the plantation of Étienne de Boré, the first mayor of New Orleans and the first person to granulate sugar, thereby helping start the sugar industry in New Orleans. The process that de Boré used was discovered by another Orleanian, Norbert Rillieux, a free man of color who was the cousin of painter Edgar Degas.

Some of the older structures of Audubon Zoo, such as the Odenheimer Sea Lion Pool and aquarium building, were built in the 1920s.

Also of note is the fact that the World's Cotton Exhibition of 1884 was held on land that is now Audubon Park. Virtually nothing tangible remains of the fair save some of the original live oaks and the faux meteorite sticking out of the golf course, said to be a huge chunk of iron ore left over from the State of Alabama exhibit.

Monkey Hill, formerly the highest elevation in the city, was not built by the WPA as is widely believed, but by the Civil Works Administration. It was completed in 1934, one year before the creation of the WPA. Earth removed from the park to build the lagoons was used to construct Monkey Hill.

No longer the highest point in the city, Monkey Hill remains one of the more universally beloved landmarks in collective civic memory. Almost every man, woman and child in New Orleans has fond memories of scaling its 'heights' and rolling down its grassy slope.

AUDUBON PARK LABYRINTH ⑦

A symbol of hope and a place of rebuilding

At the intersection of Laurel Street and East Park Drive
Tel: 504-861-2537
www.audubonnatureinstitute.org
Open: 5am–10pm
#11 Magazine Street bus

Located just outside Audubon Zoo near the Tree of Life, the labyrinth at Audubon Park is ringed by stately moss-covered oaks and sycamores, as well as commemorative benches dedicated to loved ones. The benches also provide inspirational quotes from an eclectic group including George Washington, Gandhi and Camus.

Just yards from the traffic of Magazine Street, it is all but invisible to joggers and motorists who use East Drive to traverse the park. This peaceful spot is frequented by families and individuals wishing to spend an afternoon in a natural setting.

The city's first permanent labyrinth is the result of a 5-year collaboration between the Audubon Institute and the Friends of the Labyrinth at Audubon Park. It was dedicated on Easter Sunday 2006.

The labyrinth is an ancient personal ritual shared by almost every culture. It is seen by aficionados as a universal symbol of transformation, a kind of physical medieval stroll representing life's path, and even as a link to the Godhead in some cultures. In a modern context it serves as a form of walking meditation.

Father Francois Legaux, the former Rector of Chartres Cathedral, is given credit for reviving a worldwide resurgence of interest in labyrinths in the early 1990s by drawing attention to the famous labyrinth at Chartres. He was on hand for the dedication of the Audubon labyrinth.

The labyrinth is billed by its proponents as a 'symbol of hope and a place of rebuilding, restoring and renewing'. The 2006 creation of the New Orleans labyrinth a year after Katrina's devastation seems to fit nicely into the city's belief in rebirth.

The labyrinth at Audubon Park has been designed and built by Marty Kermeen, one of the country's most renowned labyrinth builders.

LEE HARVEY OSWALD COMMEMORATIVE PLATE

The neighborhood where Oswald lived before he left for Dallas

4801 Magazine Street
Tel: 504-895-8117
Open Mond-Wed 11am-3am, Thu-Sun 11am-early morning
#11 Magazine Street bus

Affixed to the bar rail at Le Bon Temps Roulé on Magazine Street, a well worn metal plate reads: "Lee Harvey Oswald sat here."

In October of 1963, this stretch of Magazine Street in Uptown New Orleans was the neighborhood where Oswald lived before he left for Dallas and his subsequent infamy as the man most people believe assassinated President John F. Kennedy on 22 November 1963.

Now worn to the point of near illegibility, the historical plate near the far end of the bar close to the men's room replaced a plaque that sat for years on a barstool. The plate is all but ignored today by most bar patrons, who probably don't even notice its presence.

Oswald's last known residence in New Orleans is just down the street at 4905 Magazine. Le Bon Temps Roulé and Henri's Uptown Bar at 5101 Magazine were two of the main haunts associated with Oswald at that time of his life. For those in search of 4905 Magazine, the small two-room apartment, located on the side of the building, is obscured from view by a tree and a fence and is not visible from the street. However, if you travel to the address, the place is unmistakable, if a little macabre; at 4907 Magazine, which fronts the street, there is picture of John F. Kennedy sitting next to his wife Jackie in what appears to be the backseat of the presidential limousine on that fateful day.

Henry's Bar at 4400 Magazine also claims a page in Oswald's lore. He was thrown out of Henry's after asking to have the TV turned on to the local news but the TV was for exclusive sports watching. The owner refused and Oswald got miffed and was pitched out of the bar.

Another related odd touch can be found at Henry's Bar. Behind the bar, on the wall of a raised back room housing a pool table and dartboards, is a life size cardboard cutout of John Fitzgerald Kennedy.

NEUTRAL GROUND COFFEEHOUSE

A 1960s time capsule

5110 Daneel Street
Tel: 504-891-3381
www.neutralgroundcoffeehouse.com
Open: every day 7pm–Midnight
St. Charles streetcar

Closed tight during daylight hours, the multi-colored pastel wooden doorway on Daneel Street in Uptown New Orleans is the home of a rarity among American coffeehouses. It opens not in time for traditional morning coffee, but at 7pm, seven days a week.

Coffee is, in fact, not the raison d'être for the Neutral Ground; music is.

The decor has been described as funky, mellow, early flea market, laid back, eclectic and a 1960s time capsule. Indeed, the overall feel of the place is peaceful and welcoming and could almost be described as a 'found environment'.

As you enter, your visual sense is overloaded; from the barge board walls to the array of mismatched furniture, including an old sofa or two, an easy chair, picnic tables, bar stools and church pews; a pressed tin ceiling and a pillow room, which is like a suburban den meets a yurt-enclosed area in the back, tricked out with pillows.

The Neutral Ground serves neither hot food nor alcohol and is open to all ages seeking conversation or community. Its main claim to fame is music.

Seven days a week, from seven to eleven most nights, musicians book one-hour slots. The style of music tends toward folk and Americana, but you'll also find jazz, hip-hop, pop standards and rock played by a range of ages.

Many locals started out here. The coffeehouse affords amateurs and professionals alike a place to share and experiment with new songs and a live audience. The basket is passed round after the gig and many young people get the thrill of making a buck off their art for the first time.

Well known performers have played here over the years: Gina Forsyth, Jim McCormick, Lucinda Williams, Biff Rose, Pat Flory and Anders Osborne are but a few prominent locals who have gone on to successful musical careers.

The Neutral Ground started off in 1974 on Maple Street. After a fire in 1977 it became a co-op of regulars who moved to the present location in a former bar named the Red Lion. The co-op closed briefly but reopened as the Neutral Ground in 1992.

Music is not the only art form presented here. There is a poetry hour every week and a newly minted comedy hour as well. Poetry has been one of the ever-present activities here off and on since the inception of the coffeehouse, with Allen Ginsberg having read here in the early days. There is an open mic night on Sundays with 15-minute slots available on a first come first served basis.

AUDUBON PARK GOLF COURSE METEORITE

A meteor embedded in the 18th fairway?

6500 Magazine Street
Tel: 504-861-2537
www.audubonnatureinstitute.org
Open: Mon 11am–5:30pm, Tues–Thu 7am–6pm, Fri–Sun 6:30am–6pm
#11 Magazine Street bus or St. Charles streetcar

As golf hazards go, a meteorite sturdily embedded in the middle of the 18th fairway would seem to be at the top of any worldwide list of golf course oddities. Yet, there it is.

Growing up in New Orleans you are usually told that the unusual reddish rock protruding from Audubon Park Golf Course is a meteorite that fell on the city in the 19th century. But recent detective work, most notably by an academic at a local university, has claimed it to be only a relic from the World's Fair held at Audubon Park - a big chunk of iron ore left over from the state of Alabama's exhibit at there in 1884. Even as such, the chunk of iron would still be a rarity as the only artifact left that remains from the fair.

However, there are always at least two sides to every story, and in an age where conspiracy theory remains as popular as ever, there are some who invariably cling to the meteor tale. For example, a story purportedly from the *Picayune*, one of several dailies in the city at the time:

"The terrific explosion and detonation which startled all of Carrollton (a city later incorporated into New Orleans) just previous to daylight yesterday morning, shook houses and smashed panes of glass proves to have been caused by the fall of an enormous meteorite."

The story continues in another newspaper:

"Twelve lesser masses of space iron and thousands of smaller chunks and fragments scattered around the site were quickly carried away as mementos many of which still grace mantels and curiosity cabinets throughout the region."

This theory contends that the souvenir hunters posed a greater threat to the park than the space debris and it became necessary to install a fence and guards to protect the park from being trampled and carted away piece by piece. This is where the more romantic and conspiratorial version comes in. A ruse started by park officials?

However, it must be pointed out the newspaper story that first reported the landfall of the heavenly rock is datelined March 31st, one day ahead of April Fools' Day.

MIDDLE AMERICAN RESEARCH INSTITUTE GALLERY

Travel back into the antiquity of Central America

Dinwiddie Hall, Tulane University
6823 St. Charles Avenue
Tel: 504-865-5100 - www.mari.tulane.edu
Open: Mon–Fri 8:30am–4pm
Free entry
St. Charles Avenue streetcar

At the top of the stairs on the third floor of Dinwiddie Hall, one of Tulane University's oldest buildings, a small exhibit of the Middle American Research Institute Gallery (MARI) traces the history of the Maya from the pre-classic, classic and post-classic periods through to present day cultural aspects of the Maya people. The rooms are filled with items illustrating the importance of art and decorative disciplines in the life of the Maya. Beautiful examples from the MARI collection include weapons, bloodletting tools, utensils and vessels fashioned out of a variety of materials including obsidian, jade and pottery. Large bas relief copies made on the many expeditions carried out by Tulane-sponsored scholars over the course of nearly a century are highlights of the gallery, along with three-dimensional replicas of altars cast from expeditions sponsored by the institute. Detailed clay whistles in a variety of human poses and other items used by ordinary people open a window onto the importance of symbolism played in the everyday life of the Maya. The final room, dedicated to the present, highlights masks and the vibrant textiles of Guatemala, and the relevance of these items in the culture. The extensive collection is not limited, however, to Central America; its archive of photography, artifacts and field notes covers anthropology, archaeology, linguistics, ethnography and large quantities of information on Mexico, the U.S. Southwest and South America.

"The Banana Man": a highly controversial businessman at the origin of a premier Mesoamerican studies institution

The Middle American Institute was started in 1924 with money donated by Samuel Zemurray, nicknamed "Sam the Banana Man". Born Schmuel Zmurri in 1877 in what is today Moldava, Zemurray died in 1961 in New Orleans. He made his fortune in the banana trade, founding the Cuyamel Fruit Company, and later becoming head of the United Fruit Company, the world's most influential fruit company at the time (see p. 94). Both companies played highly controversial roles in the history of several Latin American countries and had significant influence on their economic and political development. The leaders of the institute had ambitious goals from the beginning and the institute has become one of the premier academic institutions in the field of Mesoamerican studies. The gallery includes tributes to scholars who played a part in the success of the institute, such as Franz Bloms, Doris Zemurray Stone, E. Wyllys Andrews V and Marcelo Canuto. In 2012 the institute opened up this new space to showcase its vast collection and to reach out to the greater community, showing why the Mesoamerican department at Tulane is held in such high regard throughout the world.

TULANE'S MUMMIES
An Egyptian mummy

Dinwiddie Hall
6823 St. Charles Avenue
Tel: 504-865-5100
www.mari.tulane.edu
Open: Mon–Fri 8:30am–4pm by special appointment
St. Charles streetcar

Unbeknownst to most people both on and off Tulane University campus, stored away in a small, tidy room in the Anthropology Department, are two mummies, one female and one male.

The small sarcophagi that once held each of the Tulane mummies occupy two top shelves. When pulled out into the light, the bottom shelf contains the splendidly preserved body of Nefer Atethu, the female mummy. The name, given to her by a Tulane professor, is translated as "beautiful young lady" in Egyptian. The male mummy, Djed-Thoth-iu-ef-ankh , whose name was discerned from papyri documentation in his sarcophagus, was autopsied and remains out of sight. He was priest and overseer of craftsmen at a Temple of Amun in Thebes.

Both mummies have had extensive medical examinations, having been X-rayed, CT scanned, and three-dimensionally digitally constructed. About 3000 years old, they are thought to have lived around 900 B.C. and were preserved in the elaborate mummification process of the New Kingdom, which suggests they were high status individuals.

The male was 50 years old at the time of his death. The female was a young girl of 16, who, it is thought, died in childbirth.

The mummies found their way to Tulane as a gift of George Gliddon, a former vice counsel to Egypt who paid looters to obtain them. He brought them to New Orleans and gave them to Tulane when he moved on to other endeavors.

Gliddon was a well-known lecturer on things Egyptian and appears as a character in the Edgar Allan Poe story *Some Words With A Mummy*.

The Tulane mummies have led a slightly Indiana Jones-ish existence since their arrival in New Orleans, having been moved around and all but forgotten several times. For almost 20 years after the Math Department moved into the building where they had been kept in glass cases, they spent their time in a dark room with no climate control under the seating area of Tulane Stadium, the site of Tulane football games, New Orleans Saints home games and three Super Bowls.

A year before the old stadium was demolished, they were moved to their new digs under the auspices of the Anthropology Department to serve as an important research tool in the field of human disease.

FREI STAINED GLASS WINDOWS AT NATIONAL SHRINE OF OUR LADY OF PROMPT SUCCOR

Perhaps the finest stained glass in the city

2635 State Street
Tel: 504-975-9627 or 504-473-6750
Open: Mon–Fri 10am until 15 minutes after mass. Sat–Sun 45 minutes before and after mass
#16 S. Claiborne Avenue bus

U pon entering the National Shrine of Our Lady of Prompt Succor chapel on the campus of Ursuline High School, you are struck by the beautiful, immaculately maintained space, with its soaring ceiling, orderly rows, exquisite wood and statuary work. But most dominant are the magnificent stained glass windows that encompass the majestic tranquility of this sacred building.

The chapel was built in 1924 shortly after the Ursulines moved from their original digs in the French Quarter. At that time, the nuns were cloistered and two chapels were built into one; a smaller chapel was put to the right of the altar so the nuns could worship out of sight of the other parishioners.

There are two sets of windows here: in the smaller chapel reserved for the nuns, the windows chronicle the life of the Virgin Mary, while the windows in the outer chapel depict events in the life of Jesus.

The windows are the work of the Émile Frei studios of St. Louis (founded in 1898) and are considered by some to be the finest stained glass in the city. Frei, a German immigrant, created and installed more windows in more New Orleans churches than anyone else.

In 1915, a large hurricane had blown out scores of church windows and when the Ursulines moved to this uptown address in the 1920s, it was a propitious time for stained glass artists.

In these windows the majesty of heaven is depicted in dark, rich tones, perhaps because powdered iron oxide fired into the colors resulted in a decidedly heavy use of blue. Frei said the windows were constructed using mouth blown glass in a process that created a thicker, more uneven glass, giving these windows "much charm".

The artistry and creativity of Frei's artisans is also enhanced by the company policy of never using the same design on any two windows.

The Ursuline order is one of the oldest institutions in New Orleans. The nuns arrived in the city in 1718 and established an educational arm for France. Their charge was to educate women and girls (including European, black, and Native American, enslaved and free alike) in literacy, numeracy and a Catholic faith - a charge they continue at the girls' high school here today.

The shadow of Jesus…

There is, as we say in New Orleans, a little lagniappe (something extra) for the faithful in the chapel: if you are near to the altar and look to your left you will see on the concrete pillar what is claimed to be the shadow of a picture of Jesus.

THE ASSUMPTION OF MARY PAINTING

The largest religious work of art on canvas in the world

Library Resource Center at Xavier University
1 Drexel Drive
Tel: 504-486-7411
www.xula.edu/library
Open: Mon–Thurs 7:30am–2am, Friday 7:30am–8pm, Saturday 10am–6pm,
Sunday 12:30pm–2am
#27 Louisiana bus or #90 Carrolton bus

Commanding the atrium in the Louisiana Library Resource Center at Xavier University, a three-storey painting of the Assumption of Mary by expressionist painter Fredrick J. Brown provides a unique blend of religious and secular imagery.

The Virgin Mary, arms outstretched in a welcoming, inclusive gesture, dominates the picture. She is flanked by two other religious figures: Pope John Paul II and Katherine Drexel, the first American Saint and founder of Xavier University, one of the most prominent African American universities in the world. The Assumption of Mary (the day that the Virgin Mary ascends to heaven) is a popular subject for painters throughout history. Many images are accompanied by depictions of a heavenly choir exalting the most holy occasion in the Catholic faith. Here at Xavier, Brown offers an interpretation that exhibits his penchant for referencing historical and urban themes, often through portraits of jazz and blues artists. His choir is a group of jazz greats with a smattering of Native Americans, slaves and Xavier workers and professors.

African American musicians including Louis Armstrong (given a spot of honor in the center of the choir), Duke Ellington, Ruby and the Romantics, Miles Davis, Dizzy Gillespie and Jimi Hendrix are among those given prominence on the canvas. Others in the choir are lesser-known or less easily recognizable stars of American music. The painting, the largest religious work of art on canvas in the world, is 28 feet wide, 33 feet high and weighs in at 6500 lbs. Its size and weight caused logistical problems demanding nothing short of a feat of engineering. The installation was supervised by John T. Scott, a sculptor, Xavier professor and Mac Arthur Grant awardee.

Xavier University is a Catholic institution that year after year is ranked among America's best private institutions of higher learning. In recent times it expanded its campus with modern facilities topped by distinctive green roofs. The building is familiar to all Orleanians as they can be seen from the busy Interstate. The campus itself, however, is located on a particularly isolated tract of land with only a few through streets. Most citizens never find themselves on the campus, making this impressive work of art very little known.

Frederick Brown is said to have been visiting New Orleans to attend the New Orleans Jazz and Heritage Festival and to see his friend, the son of Xavier's long time President Dr. Norman Francis. Dr. Francis mentioned to Brown, a world-renowned artist and the only American artist to have a major show at China's National Museum in Tiananmen Square, that he might donate one of his paintings to Xavier for the new library then under construction. Brown offered to paint a picture for Xavier and that conversation led to the huge mural now hanging in the library.

SCHOENBERGER MURAL

Once the largest continuous artistic canvas in the world

Swan River Yoga Studio
2940 Canal Street
Tel: 504-301-3134
www.swanriveryoga.com
Open: Mon–Fri 6:15am–8pm, Saturday 9:30am–9pm, Sunday 8:30am–8:30pm
Canal streetcar

Once hidden behind bookcases, plastered over, obscured from view by a drop ceiling, defaced by graffiti, and poked through with holes by workmen, "The History of Printing," a 50 foot mural finished in 1941 by Edward Schoenberger while working for the WPA, now stands almost as good as new. Expertly and lovingly restored by local artist Jeanne-Louise Chauffe, it hovers over a modern yoga studio floor.

The beautiful nine foot-tall painting follows the evolution of man's quest to chronicle his endeavors, from cave drawings to Chinese calligraphy, Egyptian hieroglyphics, medieval monks, Gutenberg, and modern printing.

New Orleans-born Schoenberger was a graduate of Warren Easton High School, which still stands across Canal Street. He left a few personal touches on his large work: the monks are said to be likenesses of family members, one a self-portrait of the artist. There is also a tiny image on one of the monks' books that is said to be Schoenberger's first wife, Philomena. For those who can get close there is also a message left by the young artist: "If you can read this, then you're too close."

Schoenberger's painting originally graced the walls here when the building served as the main branch of the New Orleans Public Library on Canal Street, a library funded by Andrew Carnegie. Schoenberger painted his work on a long sheet cemented to the wall. At the time of its completion, the canvas was said to be the largest continuous artistic canvas in the world. Schoenberger also helped paint murals on the walls of the Sazerac Bar in the Roosevelt Hotel while working for artist Paula Ninas.

The son of artistic parents, it's no surprise that Schoenberger's talents also ran to music. He not only studied art, but also attended Julliard School of Music as well as The Pratt Institute, both in New York City. He eventually left New Orleans and moved to Wausau, Wisconsin, where he served as the Marathon County Historical Museum's director until his retirement in 1980.

The new owners of the old library building, which had since been used for a variety of different business ventures, including a beauty college, were determined to restore the beautiful murals. But estimates for the work were upward of $100,000.

Enter Ms. Chauffe, a specialist in period painting and faux finishes. Chauffe worked on the restoration, often in grueling conditions and stifling New Orleans heat, finally completing the superb job in the fall of 2011.

It is said by Schoenberger's friends that he always desired his painting to be resurrected. Alas, he died in 2007 and did not see Chauffe's finished work.

JANE ALLEY

An understated tribute to New Orleans' most famous son

727 S. Broad Avenue
Tel: 504-658-8500
#39 Tulane bus

In the familiar blue and white signage of the Crescent City, the '#1 Jane Alley' street sign, erected in the middle of a municipal court plaza, memorializes the house where jazz great Louis Armstrong came into the world on August 4, 1901.

The alley was razed in the early 1960s to make way for the municipal plaza that stands there now, adjacent to the notorious Orleans Parish Prison.

A street sign may seem like an understated tribute to New Orleans' most well-known resident. But until quite recently, there has been a noticeable lack of public recognition of Mr. Armstrong's nativity. Although this has recently changed with the renaming of the International airport after the man known by musicians worldwide as 'Pops'. The commutation, along with a black marble slab of explanation, was put in the plaza during the administration of Mayor Marc Morial.

It was, and in some measure remains, a rough and tumble neighborhood located in a section of the city that was known as Backatown. In those days, the immediate blocks surrounding Armstrong's home was also referred to as 'the Battlefield' due to all the shootings and fights.

Still, when reminiscing about those formative years, Louis would say, "I had a ball growing up there as a kid." He also spoke of the influence of music on his life from an early age: "We were poor and everything, but music was all around you. Music is what kept us going."

Indeed, this milieu and the nearby neighborhood he moved to when he was around five years old was in proximity to the famous Funky Butt Hall, where presumably the young Louis would be exposed to jazz music. He would have been able to hear great musicians play, observing them by peering through the rickety walls of the building.

It can be argued that the mean streets served as an incubator to his eventual stardom. He was arrested for shooting his stepfather's pistol into the air to celebrate New Year's Eve, still a worrisome tradition in some parts of New Orleans today. Armstrong was remanded to the Colored Waif's Home for his second stint, where he came under the influence of music teacher Peter Davis. Davis taught the young Louis to play the cornet and read music.

One music historian has gone as far as saying that the arrest of the young Armstrong as a "dangerous and suspicious character" may have been the most important arrest of all time. It led Armstrong to an 18-month stay at the home and the musical mentoring of Mr. Davis.

And the rest, as they say, is history.

KING GAMBRINUS STATUE

The patron saint of beer

2600 Gravier Street
Tel: 504-821-7776
#39 Tulane Avenue bus or #94 Broad Avenue bus

Located in the former Falstaff Brewery (opened in the late 1930s), above the entrance to the Falstaff Apartments in Central City, a statue of a heroic figure holds a goblet as if to toast the city towers.

The fact that he has been standing here for the better part of 70 years on one of the tallest landmarks in the city leads many to believe that the figure, his foot propped up on a keg of beer, is the likeness of Shakespeare's Sir John Falstaff.

However, the gentleman depicted is King Gambrinus, a 12th-century nobleman considered the patron saint of beer; lore says he brewed the very first barrel of beer in the 1100s. Of course, the history books tell us that the first brew goes back a lot further, certainly a thousand years before King Gambrinus.

Still, statues of King Gambrinus were popular brewery adornments in the late 19th century and were ubiquitous at breweries all over the United States.

Although the statue has been there since the opening of the brewery, for most of its existence it was obscured by surrounding buildings, making it relatively unknown.

The statue's anonymity is ironic. It perches not far from an illuminated tower on the Falstaff Brewery building that is very familiar to generations of Orleanians. The flashing red letters that spell Falstaff lit up the city sky for the better part of the 20th century. Now that the building has been renovated into apartments, it once again serves that purpose after a few years of darkness.

If you grew up in New Orleans, you knew the messages those lights conveyed: if the globe at the top was green, the weather was fair; if red, it was cloudy; white meant showers were expected. If the letters flashed from bottom to top, this meant the temperature was rising. If Falstaff was spelled top to bottom, the temperature was falling.

BALDWIN WOOD PUMPS

One of the wonders of early 20ᵗʰ century engineering

A. Baldwin Wood No. 1 at the intersection of Broad Avenue and M. Luther King
Tel: 504- 529- 2837 (Sewerage and Water Board)
www.swbno.org
#28 MLK bus or #94 Broad bus

In the middle of Broad Avenue, where it meets Martin Luther King Boulevard, a large industrial brick building creates an island: mammoth metal tubes look as if they would be at home in a science fiction film. They actually house one of the wonders of early 20th century engineering: Baldwin Wood Number 1 Pumping Station.

Every day, thousands of Orleanians pass by on the busy thoroughfare, probably without a second thought to the integral role these pumps, working hard for over a century, have played and continue to play in the existential history of the city.

In the late 1800s, most of present-day New Orleans was swamp, not conducive to development as a residential area. This led to the city's reputation as the most unhealthy city in the nation.

In 1893, at a time when most of the city's water came from the river or rainwater cisterns, the Sewerage and Water Board was formed.

Enter A. Baldwin Wood, a Tulane graduate from New Orleans, who took a job at the newly minted S&WB, an agency he would one day lead. Using his considerable engineering talents, he invented a 12-foot screw pump designed to drain the city, the topography of which has often been described as a soup bowl.

His pumps were installed in the city between 1913 and 1915. Eventually he designed a 14-foot screw pump, many of which, such as the ones housed here, are still serving the purpose they were built to deliver.

The pumps that Wood invented were and are a marvel of sorts as only one has ever had to be repaired in over 100 years of use: he designed special rounded blades that prevented anything from being stuck in them.

In fact, when the floodwaters of Hurricane Katrina inundated the city in 2005, two of Wood's original pumps were still in use; according to those who manned those pumps during the storm, the older ones were the most reliable.

So successful were these pumps that Wood was in considerable demand from every corner of the globe for his expertise. He became a consultant but refused to leave his beloved New Orleans. Eventually he designed the drainage systems of many major North American cities, including Chicago, Milwaukee, Baltimore and San Francisco. He also designed systems in China, India and Egypt.

His most famous foreign clients were the Dutch, who studied and copied his work to accomplish the reclaiming of the Zuider Zee. Almost a century later, Dutch engineers returned to New Orleans to help rebuild the drainage system of the city.

REX DEN

The king of carnival

2531 S. Claiborne Avenue
Email: contact@rexorganization.com
Open: not generally open to the public but the sliding doors are sometimes open far enough to steal a peek
Private tours can be arranged
#16 S. Claiborne bus

The large yellow warehouse at 2351 South Claiborne Avenue is the home of one of New Orleans' most enduring symbols: this is the place where the floats for the Rex parade are built and housed between Carnival seasons.

Once upon a time, the theme of the parade, the floats and almost everything about the Rex organization (now run by The School of Design) was a secret. Times now seem to be a bit more laissez-faire.

In fact, tours are now occasionally held as fundraisers for charity - the krewe's motto *Pro Bono Publica* translates into "For the Public Good." It is also not unknown for private tours to be arranged.

Each year as soon as the parade is over (the next day in fact), the construction of next year's parade is begun. The themes and float titles are usually gleaned from history, mythology, geography and the arts, and the building of the floats consume thousands of man-hours by a small contingent of artists and artisans. All this for one day in the spotlight on Mardi Gras day.

There are a few stock floats that appear every year: the King's Float, the Boeuf Gras (a fatted calf) and the newest permanent float, the Butterfly King, added in 2012. There are a few more, but the rest of the parade is created mostly out of papier maché each year on top of old cotton wagons.

There is also an educational aspect to the krewe's work. In 2016, the total given in grants to local schools and educational groups reached $1 million, with the checks handed over at a ceremony held at the den among the floats.

Rex was started by businessmen in 1872 to welcome Grand Duke Alexis of Russia to New Orleans as well as promote tourism in New Orleans in the years after the Civil War. Two enduring aspects of New Orleans carnival started by Rex that first year were the use of purple, green and gold (the colors of Rex, which became the official colors of Mardi Gras), and the song *If Ever I Cease To Love*, a favorite of the Grand Duke's that remains the unofficial theme song of the holiday.

On Mardi Gras day, Rex is given the symbolic key to the city by the mayor of New Orleans.

The once secretive nature of the parade has also been lifted through a new outreach program: a website now provides information and links for students and teachers to learn about the subjects depicted on the floats. www.rexorganization.com.

RON MAESTRI
Contributor

- Built successful baseball program at UNO that had 14 winning seasons and nine NCAA tournament appearances during his 14-year coaching tenure

- Team finished second in the Division II World Series in 1974 and tied for fifth place in the Division I World Series in 1984

- Became athletic director for UNO in 1979 and was instrumental in the development of the university athletic complex, including Kiefer UNO Lakefront Arena and Privateer Park

Elected to the Hall of Fame in 1996

BOB ROESLER
Contributor

- Sportswriter for the *Times-Picayune* who was named sports editor in 1964 and executive sports editor in 1980

- Served on all New Orleans Super Bowl Task Force Committees, as president of the Professional Football Writer's Association, and as chairman of the Sugar Bowl Sports Selection and Hall of Fame Committees

Elected to the Hall of Fame in 1996

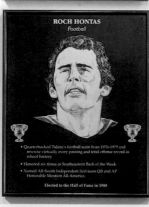

ROCH HONTAS
Football

- Quarterbacked Tulane's football team from 1976-1979 and rewrote virtually every passing and total offense record in school history

- Honored six times as Southeastern Back of the Week

- Named All-South Independent first team QB and AP Honorable Mention All-America

Elected to the Hall of Fame in 1988

EDDIE CHAMPAGNE
Football

- Lettered in track and football and was All-New Orleans Prep and All-State in football at Samuel J. Peters High School

- Named second team All-SEC, UPI third team All-American and AP honorable mention All-American in 1946

- Started for the 1949 and 1950 Los Angeles Rams Western Division championship teams

- Played for Calgary in the Canadian Football League

Elected to the Hall of Fame in 1992

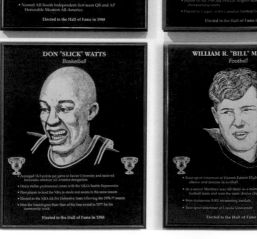

DON "SLICK" WATTS
Basketball

- Averaged 16.5 points per game at Xavier University and received honorable mention All-America recognition

- Had a stellar professional career with the NBA's Seattle Supersonics

- First player to lead the NBA in steals and assists in the same season

- Elected to the NBA All-Pro Defensive Team following the 1976-77 season

- Won the Washington State Man of the Year award in 1977 for his community work

Elected to the Hall of Fame in 1996

WILLIAM R. "BILL" MARTINEZ
Football

- Four-sport letterman at Warren Easton High School, playing both offense and defense in football

- As a senior Martinez was All-State as a member of an undefeated football team and won the state district championship

- Won numerous AAU swimming medals

- Two-sport letterman at Loyola University

Elected to the Hall of Fame in 1988

SUGAR BOWL SPORTS HALL OF FAME

The rich sporting history of New Orleans

1500 Sugar Bowl Drive
Open: varies by event
Tel: 504-828-2440
Email: info@sugarbowl.org
Rampart-St Claude streetcar

The Allstate Sugar Bowl Hall of Fame is located in the Mercedes-Benz Superdome at gate G on the Loge level right behind the escalators of the world famous sports stadium. Surprisingly, tens of thousands of football fans walk right past the attraction every year without realizing it is there.

Laser engraved likenesses attest to the feats of those who made contributions throughout the rich sporting history of New Orleans. A video screen also provides information about the inductees in alphabetical order.

Established in 1957 and sponsored by the Sugar Bowl since 1970, the Hall of Fame committee selects honorees to reflect the entire breadth of sports achievement, both on and off the field of play.

Potential inductees must be New Orleans natives who have gained significant achievements and prominence in or away from the Greater New Orleans area. Others are non-natives who made their mark in New Orleans-area sports.

The roster includes luminaries in baseball, boxing, sailing, tennis, golf, basketball, track and field, and most notably, football. The roll covers the full spectrum of the sporting universe, including coaches, officials and sportswriters, as well as athletes.

Among native sportsmen and sportswomen are baseball's Mel Ott, Rusty Staub, Mel Parnell, George Strickland and Will Clark; boxer Willie Pastrano; tennis player Linda Tuero; and football's Steve Van Buren and Hank Lauricella.

Others who found fame on the city's fields of play are coaches Eddie Robinson and Clark Shaugnessy, football's Archie Manning and Rickey Jackson, and the immortal basketball icon Pete Maravich.

MOLLY MARINE STATUE

㉑

First statue to depict a woman in military uniform in the United States

Corner of Canal Street and Elk Place
Canal streetcar

SCULPTOR
ENRIQUE ALFEREZ

MOLLY MARINE
NOVEMBER 10, 1943
"FREE A MARINE TO FIGHT"
REDEDICATED JULY 1, 1966 IN HONOR OF
WOMEN MARINES WHO SERVE THEIR COUNTRY

Just off Canal Street in the heart of New Orleans, a proud Marine in her crisp cap and ankle length skirt looks toward the horizon. Holding a pair of binoculars in a stance embodying the confidence and fortitude of America's fighting women, Molly Marine is the first statue ever to depict a woman in military uniform in the United States. The inscription at the base of the statue reads: "Free a Marine to Fight."

The statue was dedicated on 10 November 1943, the 168th birthday of the Marine Corps. New Orleans sculptor Enrique Alferez created it after a request from Marine Technical Sergeant Charles Gresham, a World War II recruiter searching for new ways to enlist women in the armed services.

Due to restrictions and the availability of materials during the war, the statue was fashioned from marble chips and granite as opposed to bronze. To keep Molly looking sharp, the statue has twice undergone restoration since its unveiling.

Marine Judy Mosgrove, a New Orleans native, was Alferez's model for what became known as "Molly Marine."

A symbol was born and the image created by Alferez has been fully embraced by the Marines. In 1999, molds were made of the Canal Street statue, and bronze replicas of the original "Molly" now stand at Marine training camps at Parris Island, SC, and Quantico, VA.

On the Wednesday of every boot camp graduation week, graduating platoons gather at the foot of the statue. The platoons hold a vote on "the recruit who best exemplified all the traits that make a Marine during recruit training," within their respective platoon. One deserving Marine from each platoon then receives the Molly Marine Award.

BASILE BARÈS PIANO

First slave to be awarded a copyright for a musical composition

130 Roosevelt Way
Tel: 504-648-1200
www.theroosevelthotel.com
Canal Street streetcar or St. Charles streetcar

O ff to one side of the lavish lobby of New Orleans' historic Roosevelt Hotel is a beautiful 19th-century rosewood baby grand piano that once belonged to Basile Barès, one of many renowned Orleanian musicians.

Built by Gaveau, one of France's foremost 19th century piano makers, the piano is notable for its intricate carving, especially on its exquisite music stand.

The city may have supplied the world with piano virtuosos for almost 200 years - such luminaries as Fats Domino, Allen Toussaint, Professor Longhair, James Booker, Dr. John, Harry Connick Jr. and even Louis Moreau Gottschalk, the famous 19th century classical composer best known for the composition 'Bamboula' - but the name Barès is not known to most.

The son of a plantation owner in New Orleans, Barès was born a slave in 1845. He grew up in the household of Adolphe Perier, the proprietor of a music emporium on Royal Street in the French Quarter, to whom Barès' mother was in servitude. Barès' affinity for the piano led him in 1860 to become the first African American, and the first slave, to be awarded a copyright for a musical composition. His work was entitled 'Grande Polka des Chasseurs à pied de la Louisiane'.

Basile also represented Mr. Perier as business agent in Paris and performed at the Paris Exhibition of 1867 to wide acclaim, some even hailing him as a musical genius.

Music was a very important part of social life in New Orleans and Barès became one of the most popular musicians in post-Civil War New Orleans.

Music historians have pointed out the influence his compositions had on the work of many more universally famous composers such as Scott Joplin and Jelly Roll Morton. Some assert that the rhythms within one of Barès' unpublished pieces, 'Los Campanillas', can be found in W.C.Handy's 'St Louis Blues'.

MYSTERY LADY TIMEPIECE

The largest of its kind ever built

Roosevelt Hotel
130 Roosevelt Way entrance
Tel: 504-648-1200
www.therooseveltneworleans.com
Canal Street streetcar

The Waldorf Astoria hotel chain has a policy of including a signature clock in the lobby of all its properties. The Roosevelt Hotel, part of this chain, is no exception. Entering the luxurious lobby from Roosevelt Way, an extraordinary conical pendulum clock stands on a block of Algerian onyx in the center of the arcade. It has a bronze statue of a woman holding a golden scepter with a rotating silver globe, which serves as the driving force of the timepiece.

The mechanism operates via a weight fixed on the end of a string suspended from a pivot. It is similar to an ordinary pendulum clock but instead of swinging back and forth, the pendulum moves in a circle with the rod or string tracing out a cone shape. This provides a smoother and quieter movement.

Built in Paris, the Mystery Lady Timepiece clock was created and designed by one of France's greatest clock makers of the 19th century, E. Farcot.

This clock is the largest of its kind ever built and was exhibited by Farcot at the Paris Exhibitions of 1867 and 1878. These exhibitions were the equivalent of a World's Fair and provided an opportunity for artisans to advertise their wares to countless thousands. The fact that this clock was displayed at two exhibitions is an indication of its importance; only the finest specimens of a given artform were accepted.

The bronze lady by Albert-Ernest Carrier de Belleuse (1824-1887), who was considered the finest French sculptor of the 19th century, adds to the cache of the piece. A teacher of Auguste Rodin, Carrier de Belleuse is known for many works of note, including the "Torches" commissioned by Napoleon III, which now flank the staircases at the Paris Opera House.

These types of clocks are called "Mystery Clocks" because the mechanism is hidden in the base of the figure (in this case the bronze lady).

JEFFERSON HIGHWAY MARKER

From inception to abandonment in just 20 years

Corner of St. Charles Avenue and Common Street
St. Charles streetcar

The blue Georgia granite obelisk at the corner of St. Charles Avenue and Common Street stands in plain view in the Central Business district, historically one of the busiest areas of the city. However, despite the prominence of this unusual six-foot-tall marker, dedicated in 1917 to highlight the spot where the early national highway ended, it goes largely unnoticed. It is true that you could live a very full life in New Orleans and still not be aware of its existence.

The commemorative plaque says "the End of Jefferson Highway New Orleans to Winnepeg". The marker was the gift of the Daughters of the American Revolution in 1917 and was an important enough structure at the time to have both the mayor of New Orleans, Martin Behrman, and the Governor of Louisiana, R.S. Pleasant, on hand for the ceremony.

The Jefferson Highway was an important route from north to south and was built in the spirit of the famous East–West Lincoln Highway.

The rapid march of technology, along with the rapid change that it brings, is evident in the brief history of the Jefferson Highway.

The first documented trans-continental automobile trip was taken in 1903 from San Francisco to New York. That the Jefferson Highway was built just seven years later only to end in the late 1920s speaks of the efficient reaction to the automobile by the United States in building modern roads to accommodate this transportation revolution. The highway's journey from inception to abandonment in less than 20 years in some ways mirrors the swift changes in technology in the 21st century.

Some parts of the Jefferson Highway, nicknamed at the time 'The Palms to Pine Highway', still exist and many stretches still bear the name. Notably, much of Jefferson Highway in Jefferson Parish from Shrewsbury Road to Kenner is familiar to all residents of the area as Jefferson Highway.

The federal road, an early ancestor of the Interstate system, in theory once ran through major cities such as New Orleans, Shreveport, Joplin, Kansas City, Des Moines and Minneapolis, ending in Winnipeg, Canada, covering over 2,400 miles and passing through 289 cities.

UNITED FRUIT FORMER HEADQUARTERS

25

One of the most powerful and controversial corporations in United States history

321 St. Charles Avenue
St. Charles Avenue streetcar

At 321 St. Charles Avenue in New Orleans Central Business District, an elaborate masonry doorway of two fruit-filled cornucopias is crowned by a basket full of fruit above intricate ornamentation proclaiming 'United Fruit 1920'. This was once the headquarters of one of the most powerful and controversial corporations in United States history. Today the building houses a savings and loans office, but the backstory linked to this place reaches into New Orleans, regional and world history. United Fruit was founded in 1899 in Boston and found its way to New Orleans via Samuel Zemurray, a larger-than-life businessman born in what is now Moldavia. Zemurray, known as Sam the Banana Man, rose from poverty through the business he built with a $190 investment in bananas. He sold his Cuyamel Fruit Company to United Fruit (his biggest competitor) in 1930. After watching the company fall

on hard times a few years later, he came out of retirement and gained control of United Fruit Company in a hostile takeover, moving its headquarters to New Orleans.

Once one of the most powerful corporations on earth, United Fruit was basically the de facto ruler of several Central American countries. The company was always politically controversial, leading prominent Latin American writers such as Gabriel García Márquez and Pablo Neruda to dub United Fruit "El Pulpo" or "The Octopus" (see image). Zemurray himself once organized and carried out a coup to take over the government of Honduras in 1910 to protect his company's interests. The coup was planned and launched from New Orleans and carried out by, among others, Guy "Machine Gun" Molony, a former New Orleans police chief. Sam Zemurray was also an active philanthropist, contributing heavily to Tulane University and politicians such as FDR. He was also a significant benefactor of liberal magazine *The Nation*.

Zemurray and the Exodus *ship to Palestine*

Zemurray, a non-practicing Jew, was a large contributor to Israel. Through meetings with Chaim Weizman in the 1920s, Zemurray contributed (mostly anonymously) large sums of money to help the Zionist cause. He is in fact thought to have given money to purchase the ship *Exodus*, which, had a Panamaniam registry. Although the *Exodus* was unsuccessful in landing refugees in Palestine, the plight of the ship raised world awareness of the cause. Between 1946 and 1948, Zemurray is thought to have paid for 37,000 Jews to resettle from Europe to the new state of Israel.

Another link to United Fruit can be found further up river on St. Charles Avenue: the beautiful white-columned mansion that now serves as the residence of Tulane University's president was once home to Sam the Banana Man.

"Banana republic"

The term 'banana republic' was inspired by the policies and actions of corporations such as United Fruit. It was coined in a short story by O. Henry, who launched his writing career during a short stay in the Crescent City while on the lam from embezzlement charges in Texas, before traveling to Honduras on one of Sam Zemurray's banana boats.

FEDERAL RESERVE MUSEUM

26

A sleek, modern exploration of money

525 St. Charles Avenue
Tel: 504-593-5857
www.frbatlanta.org/about/tours/nola/museum.aspx
Open: Mon–Fri 9am–4pm
Free entry
St. Charles streetcar

Located in the Federal Reserve Building, the Museum of Trade, Finance, and the Fed is a sleek, modern exploration of money, trade, the Federal Reserve System and how it relates to New Orleans' place in the development of these ideas throughout history.

Visitors are given a plastic bag of shredded currency before the tour begins, as one of the jobs of the Federal Reserve Bank is to take worn and tattered currency out of circulation.

A self-guided tour starts with a video. An enlarged silver certificate wraps around the screen and the video describes the history of currency; from barter to the first coinage in Lydia, Minore Asia, to the world's first national bank in the Netherlands in the 1600s.

The next stop on the tour is a high-tech touch screen that allows visitors to create their own currency, complete with their picture on the bill. After completing the design you can then email the image to yourself.

As you continue around the room, New Orleans' contributions in the field of banking and finance are highlighted with brief biographies of individuals who played significant roles in New Orleans becoming an important financial center. You then move on to a small case containing the actual currencies used in the city, such as Spanish silver reales and U.S. trimes. Another large wraparound note, this time a replica of a Citizens Bank of Louisiana dix note (the derivative of the term "Dixie") highlights currency used in Louisiana; all the way from fur pelts to

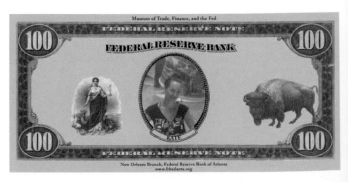

Spanish silver, French playing cards briefly used in lieu of money, and finally the Federal Reserve notes we use today.

The tour, which takes about a half hour, ends with two touchscreen displays: one offers a choice of financial subjects relating to Federal Reserve history; the other gives you a chance to test your new-found knowledge of monetary issues.

In an ironic twist, this branch in New Orleans is just across St. Charles Avenue in Lafayette Square. A bust of the great American statesman Henry Clay sits in the square, his eyes seemingly focused on the Federal Reserve Building. Ironic because, along with President Andrew Jackson, then-senator Clay was initially one of the chief opponents of a central bank for the United States, only to change his mind and become one of the most ardent supporters of the Second Bank of the United States, considered a predecessor of the Federal Reserve.

PIAZZA D'ITALIA

One of America's little known architectural gems

Lafayette Street
St. Charles streetcar
www.americanitalianculturalcenter.com
#11 Magazine Street bus

For all its magnificence and artistic pedigree, the Piazza d'Italia sits all but abandoned in the heart of a city block in New Orleans Central Business District, little more than a ruin twice over.

This award winning urban space consists of a public fountain in the shape of the Italian peninsula surrounded by multiple hemicyclic colonnades, a clocktower, a campanile and a Roman temple rendered in neon, slate, stone and stainless steel. It is a truly stunning sight. Yet the abstract minimalist work sits ignored but for the occasional visitor who stumbles across it or street people who use it as a respite from the din of the city around them.

The piazza is a surprise to many Orleanians who happen upon it. Stepping through the gates at Lafayette and Commerce Streets in the Central Business District, visitors generally find they have this beautifully conceived work of urban design to themselves. It's easy to understand the bewilderment at the reason for its existence and abandonment.

The space was initially conceived as a permanent public commemoration of the substantial Italian-American community's contribution in the city. It was designed and completed in 1978 by postmodern architect Charles Moore, former dean of Yale's architecture school, whose face is prominently displayed on the work. The piazza was hailed as an architectural masterpiece even before its completion.

Alas, the piazza began to deteriorate almost immediately. Rave reviews spoke of it in glowing terms such as 'witty' and 'exuberant', but the space did not capture the imagination of the city. Its failure to achieve its potential was blamed on a variety of factors, including an economic downturn and the fact that it was surrounded by towering office buildings, leaving it hidden in a valley of skyscrapers. A mere nine years after its debut it was in need of serious restoration. It became known as the first postmodern ruin.

After a recent a restoration the space has sadly gone to seed once again.

But even in its anonymity it is still beautiful and can truly be described as one of America's little known architectural gems - an exquisite idea biding its time for rediscovery.

ITALIAN AMERICAN MUSEUM

The French Quarter was essentially an Italian enclave

537 South Peters Street
Tel: 504-522-7294
www.americanitalianculturalcenter.com
Open: Tue–Fri 10am–4pm
Entry fee: Adults $8, Seniors $5, Children under 12 free
#10 Tchoupitoulas bus

 New Orleans is not generally associated with Italians as much as it is with French, Spanish and African Americans, but Italians are one of the major ethnicities in the city. In fact, in the early 20th century, the French Quarter was essentially an Italian enclave.

Housed in an old brick façade with Italian and American flags pointing out toward the river in New Orleans' historic commercial district (now known as the CBD), the Italian American Museum chronicles the journey, travails, successes and triumphs of New Orleans' extensive Italian American community.

Exhibits take the visitor on a journey beginning in Sicily, from where the great majority of New Orleans' Italian community can trace their families: they came to America in great waves in the 1880s, driven from their homeland by economic hardship.

New Orleans was an important destination for Italians from Sicily, many specifically from the Palermo area. One of the reasons for this was the similar climate that Sicily and New Orleans shared. In addition, Palermo was a thriving citrus center, as was southern Louisiana.

If you look at the map of Sicily displayed here, you will see surnames that are very familiar in New Orleans. When new immigrants arrived, customs agents often simplified matters for them by giving them the name of the towns from where they came. A new home often meant a new name and life.

The early arrivals to New Orleans established many Benevolent Associations to supply insurance, health care and other services that were not always available to immigrants. Many of these remain viable to the present day. These societies were brought together to create the Cultural Center, raising awareness of the great contribution made to the city by its Italian community.

The museum houses exhibits ranging from the immigrants' struggle to adapt and be accepted in their new home to the importance of family, highlighted by photographs taken of whole families. Food and religion come together in a very fine reconstruction of a St. Joseph altar, a New Orleans tradition brought from Sicily.

A wall is also dedicated to the infamous "Who Killa da Chief" episode, in which police chief David Hennessey was murdered. Though no one was convicted, Italians were blamed and several were subsequently lynched by a citizen mob. Italy and the United States almost went to war over this incident and it was only averted when the United States government paid reparations to the families of the men who were killed.

Many modern Americans of Italian descent show a new curiosity and interest in the old country, so today, the Italian Cultural Center where the museum is located serves as the hub of many activities such as lectures, films, and Italian lessons.

ALBRIZIO MURAL AT UNION PASSENGER TERMINAL

Four hundred years of Louisiana history

1001 Loyola Avenue
Tel: 504 -528-1612
Open: 5am–10pm
Rampart-St Claude streetcar

The enormous colorful fresco towering over the waiting area of the Union Passenger Terminal in downtown New Orleans was painted by Conrad Albrizio in the style of great Mexican muralists of the 20th Century. The four large panels, each 60 feet long and 8 feet high, represent the history of the Crescent City in four distinct eras: exploration, colonization, conflict and the modern age. The huge masterwork was completed in 1954 in time for the grand opening of the then state-of-the-art passenger terminal.

The painting covers 2,166 square feet and is a mixture of artistic styles, featuring impressionistic and cubist elements. Its vibrant colors are balanced by muted shadows of earthy tones and brooding moods that capture the richness of the state and city's history.

Albrizio traveled to Mexico in the 1950s, where he studied mosaics. This influence jumps from this work as do the social and political messages portrayed. Its themes cover 400 years of Louisiana and New Orleans history.

At one time every Orleanian was very familiar with the vibrant mural that dominates the waiting hall, but as time marches on, train and bus travel have become more rare, and the murals have become a hidden treasure. Relatively few contemporary New Orleanians have seen this stunning work, or are even aware of its existence.

Albrizio was born in 1894 in New York City and came to Louisiana after receiving his first large commision to create work for Huey Long's new art deco capitol building in Baton Rouge. He was a longtime art professor at Louisiana State University and created numerous public works all over Louisiana and Alabama.

At the time of its completion the mural in the Union Passenger Terminal was one of the largest in the United States. It was recently refurbished by the New Orleans Building Corporation, which will allow future generations to enjoy and marvel at this true New Orleans treasure.

"EMBRACING THE DREAM" SCULPTURE

An abstract sculpture as a tribute to Martin Luther King Jr.

Corner of Oretha Haley Castle and Martin Luther King Jr. Boulevards
#15 Freret bus

In Central City, two avenues bear the names of civil rights activists: one a local, Oretha Haley Castle, and the other, Dr. Martin Luther King Jr. At the intersection of the two stands an abstract sculpture as a tribute to Dr. King. The statue was created by Frank Hayden, a distinguished professor from Southern University, the largest black university in the world.

At first glance, the avant-garde appearance of the statue may cause confusion about its meaning. That was certainly the case at its unveiling, when most in attendance expected the memorial to be a traditional likeness of the civil rights icon. The initial reaction to the work was mixed at best. The sculpture is a green egg-shaped design, with arms and hands reaching out from the edges toward each other.

Hayden explained that the work, entitled "Embracing the Dream," represented life and growth, with the arms and hands reaching out for brotherhood. Inside the egg are passages from Dr. King's speeches. There is also a bullet hole in the design, representing his assassination.

The location of the monument is appropriate from a historical perspective; it sits at a former hub of commercial activity on the previously named Dryades Street, once a thriving mercantile corridor of over 200 Jewish and African-American businesses.

The Southern Christian Leadership Conference that Dr. King led was founded in Central City, and the annual parade to honor Dr. King passes through what is still a predominantly African-American neighborhood.

Time has taken its toll on the area but in recent years the corridor of Oretha Haley Castle Blvd., named after a college student who participated in many civil rights protests in the city, has been the focus of urban revitalization.

In fact, just across the street, the memorial faces two new gleaming additions to the streetscape: the Southern Food and Beverage Museum recently moved into its new modern digs, and on the other corner is the New Orleans Jazz Orchestra, a facility that strives to act as an entertainment and education resource for the community.

Oretha Haley Castle Blvd. has been designated a National Accredited Main Street and has been recognized on the National Register of Historic Districts.

"CITYWATCH"

Five bunnymen looking out onto the city

1228 Oretha Haley Castle Blvd.
#28 M.L. King bus

If you look up while driving down Oretha Haley Castle Boulevard and think you see men in bunny suits peering down from the roof, you're not imagining things. This is a work of art entitled 'Citywatch' by New Orleans artist Alex Podesta.

Podesta, who says the work is a homage to Rodin's 'Burghers of Calais', wanted his work to have a very personal touch, so he used a mold of his own features to create the faces of each of the five bunnymen. The mold is a plastic composite which is polished, painted and attached to an armature of wood covered with Styrofoam. The artist says his work is meant to be humorous but thought provoking; because he is part of each bunny he feels there is a strong element of introspection.

Born in North Carolina, Podesta made his way to New Orleans through a culinary job using skills he learned from his mother while growing up on a chicken farm. He contends this rural childhood was where the bunny idea was born.

His artistic skills come naturally. His grandfather worked with famed filmmaker Luis Buñuel and his grandmother, also an artist, worked with Diego Rivera. He remembers as a child receiving tools for Christmas rather than toys, encouraging his spatial and building talents and leading him to earn his MFA in sculpting from the University of New Orleans.

Podesta has more bunnymen, which each take two to three hundred hours to complete, lying prone in the lobby of the Saratoga Building on Loyola Avenue. He once had two bunnymen half-submerged in the Grand River in Michigan.

The bunnymen were originally to be displayed at Bayou St. John, but city permitting problems led the pieces first to the new Falstaff apartment building then to the roof on Oretha Haley Castle in 2008, where they can be seen today.

K&B PLAZA

*One of the most important and idiosyncratic
collections of modern and contemporary art*

*1055 St. Charles Avenue
Tel: 504-586-2011
Open: Mon–Fri 8am–4 pm
St. Charles streetcar*

P artially obscured from the busy thoroughfare just below the K&B Plaza (the former corporate headquarters of K&B, an iconic local drugstore chain) and shielded from view by a retaining wall, a sculpture garden gathers a collection of ten museum quality sculptures that ring the building. A granite fountain sculpture by Isama Noguchi, 'The Mississippi', dominates this island of solitude one storey above St. Charles Avenue at Lee Circle.

The plaza, however, holds only a small portion of the Sydney and Walda Besthoff sculpture collection, the bulk of which was moved to the Sydney and Walda Besthoff Sculpture Garden now next to the New Orleans Museum of Art.

But the art doesn't stop at the plaza; the former corporate headquarters building contains and displays a world class collection of modern and contemporary art in the lobby and on the walls of the first floor. On the 7th floor more of the collection can be seen by the public, in one of the corridors that now serve as the offices of the remnants of the K&B corporation.

The Sydney and Walda Besthoff collection has been called the one of the most important and idiosyncratic collections of modern and contemporary art assembled in the past 20 years. It provides a survey of modern art expressed in painting, sculpture, objects and photography.

Notable specialties of the collection are its Photorealist works; this school of art originated in the 1970s, coinciding with the beginnings of the Besthoff collection. Paintings here include works by pioneers of the genre such as Richard Estes, Ralph Goings and Audrey Flack, as well as more recent artists such as R.E. Penner and Davis Cone.

The collection also has a distinctive New Orleans flavor; one of the mission statements of the foundation is to promote and encourage New Orleans based artists. Local artists of note included in the collection are Robert Gordy, George Dureau, Ida Kohlmayer and Alan Gerson among others.

Designed and built for the John Hancock Insurance Company in 1962 by Skidmore, Owings and Merril, the building was the recipient of design awards. It was purchased in 1972 by Sydney Besthoff to serve as the corporate headquarters of K&B. It is said that one of the defining reasons for the purchase of this building was the presence of the Noguchi sculpture on the plaza.

When the Greater New Orleans Bridge was expanded and the government threatened to take the building by eminent domain, K&B cut a deal to save the building and the plaza, which is very close to the elevated interstate, by installing specially designed reflectors to prevent the building's lights from blinding drivers.

PATRICK F. TAYLOR LIBRARY AT THE ㉝ OGDEN MUSEUM OF SOUTHERN ART

One of the most spectacular interiors in New Orleans

925 Camp Street
Tel: 504-539-9650
www.ogdenmuseum.org
Open: Mon, Wed, Fri, Sat, Sun 10am–5pm, Thurs 10am–8pm. Closed Tuesday
St. Charles streetcar

Unknown to most people, the Patrick F. Taylor Library at the Ogden Museum of Southern Art boasts one of the most spectacular interiors in New Orleans. A reading room of the formerly named Charles T. Howard Library was opened in 1889 and closed to the public in 1939, and only recently have renovations started to transform the space back to its original beauty.

The huge circular room has a 40 foot-high ceiling and a rotunda measuring 40 feet in diameter with a massive masonry fireplace. Seventeen oak hammer beams stick out above the floor with carved stylistic wolves reaching toward the center of the room. Viewed from below, the beams curve up and merge, creating an intricate radial pattern.

The building's exterior also stands out as unique in the New Orleans architectural landscape. It is the only work in the city from a design by Henry Hobson Richardson. Richardson's association with the buildings and his importance in American architechture is all but unknown by average Orleanians.

Richardson left New Orleans at the outbreak of the Civil War to study at Harvard and later excelled as a student at L'École des Beaux Arts in Paris. He went on to design and build many distinctive buildings in the north such as Trinity Church in Boston, which was named the most outstanding building in the United States in 1885 by *American Architecture and Builders Magazine*.

His style, known as Richardsonian Romanesque, is characterized by huge, heavy stone façades, squat towers, Romanesque arches, banded windows and recessed entrances. The reddish brick and Massachusetts sandstone exterior of the Patrick F. Taylor Library is classic Richardson, and it is the only structure of his design in the southern United States.

The original building was donated by noted local philanthropist Patrick Taylor and is now part of the Ogden Museum of Southern Art, started by Roger Ogden, who donated his extensive collection of southern art to the University of New Orleans Foundation. The museum now houses the largest, most significant collection of southern art in the world and is the first Louisiana museum to be an affiliate of the Smithsonian.

The library can be rented for special events like weddings and fundraisers. It is connected to the museum by a tunnel and is not always open to the public.

CONFEDERATE MEMORIAL HALL MUSEUM

The oldest operating museum in Louisiana

929 Camp Street
Tel: 504-523-4522
www.confederatemuseum.com
Open: Tues–Sat 10am–4pm
St. Charles streetcar

Guarded by a large cannon mounted on a terrace Just a block away from the National World War II museum, the reddish-brown Richardsonian Romanesque terracotta building on Camp Street is home to the Confederate Memorial Hall Museum, a depository of memorabilia from the bloodiest conflict in United States history, the American Civil War. The interior of the small but stately museum boasts dark cypress paneling and exposed ceiling beams, beautifully complimenting the cypress wood and glass cases packed with treasured artifacts from the conflict. Much of the trove was donated by the families of the war's participants, which gives the place a historic yet very personal feel.

The collection is the second largest of Confederate-related items in existence, behind only the American Civil War museum in Richmond, Virginia. It is comprised of all the accoutrements of soldiers at war: uniforms, swords, pistols, rifles and ordinance, along with more personal items such as pipes, bibles, diaries, boots, photographs, portable writing desks, letters, and even a wooden chess set.

Many prominent actors in the war from the Confederate side - Robert E. Lee, Stonewall Jackson, Braxton Bragg, P.G.T. Beauregard and Jefferson Davis - are among those represented by personal effects donated by their families. A display case to the rear of the hall contains several items donated by Varia Howell Davis, the widow of Jefferson Davis who died in New Orleans in 1889. His embroidered butterfly-adorned slippers, uniforms, his Bible and a letter and gifts from Pope Pius IX sent to Davis while he was incarcerated after the war are all here. Davis was laid in state at the hall and it is estimated that 60,000 people came to view his body. This is an indication of the fervency of the emotion that many citizens of the 'Lost Cause' held onto nearly 25 years after the war's end.

One of the main missions of the museum is the remembrance of Louisiana residents' participation in the conflict, as well as the remembrance of military battles and campaigns that occurred on Louisiana soil. It is estimated that 66,000 Louisiana citizens served in the war, 15,000 of whom died.

Memorial Hall, the oldest operating museum in Louisiana, opened in 1891. It was the donation of New Orleans philanthropist Frank T. Howard in memory of his late father, Charles T. Howard, a veteran of the Confederate army. Frank Howard had the building that houses the museum designed and built to fit in with the architecture of the Howard Memorial library, which still stands adjacent to the present day museum.

As one moves through the collection, the feeling of the personal toll on families is palpable, particularly in the case of the belongings of Charles Horton, who died at the Battle of Mansfield. His mess kit has an inscription in the wooden handle of his fork that simply says, "To a good boy".

PORT OF NEW ORLEANS PLACE

One of the most intimate views of the Mississippi

1350 Port of New Orleans Place
Tel: 504-522-2551
www.portno.com
Riverfront streetcar or #10 Tchoupiltoulas bus

Even though it stands in the heart of New Orleans, the striking 30 foot-tall statue named "Mother River" is one of the least known sculptures in the city. Orleanians are often taken completely by surprise that such a large work of art, as well as the plaza itself, even exists.

The plaza is located in front of the building that is home to the Port of New Orleans, hidden out of sight and mind between the mammoth Ernest Morial Convention Center and the Mississippi River. The area is only seen by those with business at the Port offices or by those passing on the river.

Along with the large green statue, the plaza also has several planters containing flourishing satsuma bushes replete with fruit. The Mississippi River is but 30 feet away from eight wooden swings, each big enough to hold two adults, facing one of the most intimate views of the Mississippi to be found inside the city limits.

To the left of the swings is a most unique view of the two big Mississippi River bridges that cross the water. This is a rare vantage point that most will never see.

The statue itself is of a mother figure, her outstretched arms symbolizing the source of the river and, according to the plaque at its base, the power, beauty and history of the Mississippi. The robes of the figure are the many tributaries (such as the Ohio and Missouri) of the vast watershed that extends almost from the Canadian border to the Gulf of Mexico. The bas-reliefs at the base depict tugs, river vessels and working men and women of the river.

Dedicated in 2001, the statue – a survivor of Hurricane Katrina – is the work of artist Joseph Cleary and New Orleans architect Arthur O. Davis.

Cleary is an important artist of the last half of the 20th century with a varied and distinguished career as a working artist and teacher. He started out by drawing pin-up portraits in crayon for his fellow Merchant Marines, eventually becoming a very well known and successful illustrator for magazines such as the *Saturday Evening Post, Good Housekeeping, Ladies Home Journal, Boy's Life* and *Argosy*. Cleary worked as a successful commercial artist on numerous magazine advertisements, utilizing a unique style that many would recognize even if they did not know his name.

DOLLHOUSE MUSEUM

A meticulously planned and furnished collection

2200 St. Charles Avenue
Tel: 504-494-2200
www.houseofbroel.com
Open: Mon–Sat 11am–3:30pm
Entry fee (by appointment only): Adults $10, Children $5
St. Charles streetcar

S t. Charles Avenue is home to many fine houses from a bygone era and the stately mansion at 2220 St. Charles is a fine example. But what many people don't know is that this home also hosts dozens of dollhouses, which are part of a museum created with great care and passion by Bonnie Broel.

The dollhouses, which occupy the better part of the second floor, fill rooms with furnishings and dolls, their adherence to Americana reminiscent of scenes right out of a Currier and Ives print. Others have a distinctly exotic theme, such as the beautiful Chinese dollhouse with mini Oriental furniture and decorations. Broel's pièce de résistance, her final dollhouse, is a Russian palace, standing 10 feet high by 12 feet wide. It took five and half months to build and 10 years to gather all the interior bells and whistles. The Russian palace has a personal connection for Broel, the daughter of a Polish nobleman. The family's estate was in Russia - a picture of it hangs prominently on the wall of Broel's office. Her father fought for the Tsar's army in World War I before finding his way to America. Like many things, this passion for dollhouses started by happenstance. Broel and her young son Clark attended a school fundraiser with a dollhouse display. Her son mused that it might be fun to construct a dollhouse, comparing it to model airplanes he had assembled. The mother and son team waded right in by first doing a practice dollhouse, a small sweetshop that you can see at the museum today.

Broel says she was instantly hooked on her new hobby. The next project was a Tudor House that took six months to complete. The collection now consists of 12 large houses and over 30 room vignettes, all meticulously planned and furnished.

As if this fascinating attraction weren't enough, there is another curious tale embedded in Ms. Broel's domain: on the walls of her office are framed displays of labels of a product her father produced during the Great Depression. The product's existence has been shrouded from general knowledge by time. The American Frog Canning Company on Jefferson Highway in Jefferson Parish was started by Broel's father, and flourished up until right before World War II. To honor her father, Broel has a large collection of frog figures, some of which she acquired for him, others that were given to her by friends who knew of the connection.

On the third floor there is still more. Ms. Broel has a small fashion museum that displays her work as a seamstress and designer. The museum includes beautiful apparel she created for Orleanians and celebrities such as Anne Rice and Sandra Bullock.

NEW ORLEANS FIRE DEPARTMENT MUSEUM

The last New Orleans firehouse to switch from horse-drawn wagons to motorized vehicles

1135 Washington Avenue
Tel: 504-658-4713
miwilliams@nola.gov
Open: Mon–Fri 9am–2pm by appointment
#11 Magazine Street bus

O n a shaded avenue in Uptown New Orleans, an old firehouse, which first opened in 1850s, has the distinction of being the last New Orleans firehouse to switch from horse-drawn wagons to motorized vehicles. It has now found new life as home to the New Orleans Fire Department Museum, a depository of old fire trucks and other memorabilia that gives a glimpse into the rich history of firefighting in New Orleans and the United States.

Prominent among the artifacts is antique fire equipment: an 1838 Hunneman Hand Pumper, 1896 Ahrens 2nd Class Steamer, and a 1927 Ahrens Fox-MS2 sporting a dramatic silver ball to hold air and smooth outgoing pressure from the pump.

There is also a Civil War-era hand drawn ladder truck and an 1859 Gamewell Fire Alarm Telegraph.

The old firehouse holds a nice collection of fire helmets from around the world, including a metal one from Italy resembling something worn by a Roman Centurion, and modern versions that appear more suitable for super heroes than firemen.

Other curiosities include early fire extinguishers, cypress wood water mains, hand pulled chemical carts from the 1890s, old uniforms and an assortment of obsolete communication equipment.

The second floor of the museum is in the space once reserved for bunking down, as evidenced by the fire poles that firefighters used to slide down to the trucks. Video presentations made by the New Orleans Fire Department chronicle the life of today's firefighters and also tell the story of the heroic and varied roles played by the NOFD during Katrina, including footage of the very first time helicopters were ever used to fight fires in an urban setting.

The museum opened in 1995 and officially has never closed, not even during Katrina, as some firefighters actually sat out the storm here.

The museum and its related activities now serve many purposes aside from the tours that are available by appointment. It hosts hundreds of school children each year and is charged with, among other functions, the promotion of safety education, recruitment, public relations and even Mardi Gras parade participation via a refurbished vintage 1896 fire truck - the last horse-drawn steam engine that went out of service in 1922.

38

IRISH CHANNEL TINY MUSEUM

A tiny museum

2923 Constance Street
Open: 24 hours a day, although avoid visiting late at night as it is in front of a private residence
#11 Magazine Street bus

At 2923 Constance Street, a tiny yellow wooden box, similar to the small free libraries popping up in many residential areas, proclaims "A Tiny History of the Irish Channel (a tiny museum)."

Open the swinging door held closed by a wooden peg and you'll find a concise story that charts a swift history of the Irish Channel, one of New Orleans' more legendary neighborhoods.

The first settlers of the high ground near the Mississippi River that now constitutes the Irish Channel were Native Americans who inhabited the area over 3000 years ago. Among the tribes were the Tchoupitoulas (pronounced *chop-a-tool-us*), translated as 'river people,' from whom the street gets its name.

As you turn the dioramas, which revolve on a base fashioned from a Dexter Gordon LP, text and pictures fast forward to the arrival of Europeans to these environs. Particular focus is on the Livaudais Plantation, which occupied the tract where the Irish Channel now stands, and the significant impact that slavery had in the economic success of New Orleans.

As the 19th century moved along, the plantation was sold off one parcel at a time and soon waves of immigrants entered New Orleans here. The Irish Channel is bounded by the Mississippi and as European immigrants began pouring into the growing city and its bustling port, workers who landed in the city found cheap places to live closer to the river.

These immigrants included Germans and many Irishmen, who then joined the African American citizens after the Livaudais Plantation had been sold off. Eventually, German and Italian immigrants added another element to this thriving working class neighborhood.

The Channel gets its name from the fact that at one time in the middle of the 19th century, New Orleans had the largest Irish population in the American South. The Irish are given credit for the creation of a New Orleans stalwart, the shotgun house, facilitated by long narrow lots carved out of plantation properties. Another Irish 'creation' that also has distinctive German roots is the unique New Orleans 'brogue' or, as it is known these days, "Yat," the distinct New Orleans dialect and accent that many compare to the New York accent.

The final exhibit in the tiny museum addresses post-Katrina with a scene of a communal South Louisiana ritual, the crawfish boil.

39

GARGOYLE AT JACKSON AVENUE

One claw hand brandishing a Medusa-like head

709 Jackson Avenue
#10 Tchoupitoulas street bus

At 709 Jackson, looming high over the Lower Garden District, a menacing quasi-human beast hangs from the side of a converted synagogue that is now an apartment building. The gargoyle holds the bricks with one claw hand while the other brandishes a severed Medusa-like head, presumably to menace the populace below; the owner of the building is said to have installed the gargoyle to scare off vandals.

This modern gargoyle is the work of Thomas Randolph Morrison, a sculptor whose first gargoyle appeared on the bell tower of St. Vincent's Guesthouse on Magazine Street, where Morrison had a studio. That gargoyle was torn down by a vandal during Mardi Gras week in 2016.

Morrison's first venture into sculpting was working in Hollywood creating figures for Walt Disney Films. He also worked with master movie theme park sculptor Leo Rijn. But he became weary of life in California and moved to New Orleans, finding a special space at St Vincent's. Morrison's talents were well suited to the needs of Mardi Gras and he worked for several years making floats for some of the more prominent Carnival krewes.

Constructed from lightweight foam reinforced with steel and covered in fiberglass, Morrisson's all-weather gargoyle weighs in at about 15lbs and is built to be attached to chimneys and walls.

Gargoyles have been installed on buildings for centuries for adornment and perhaps as warnings. The word gargoyle is derived from the French word 'gargouille', meaning 'throat' or 'gullet'. The classic gargoyle's purpose was as a spout to get rid of rainwater. The gurgling sound of the water no doubt led to the name.

GERMAN AMERICAN CULTURAL CENTER

By 1860, New Orleans' population was one sixth German

519 Huey P. Long Avenue
Tel: 504-363-4202
www.gacc-nola.org
Open: Wed–Sat 10am–3pm
Free entry
W2 Westbank Expressway bus

Towering over old downtown Gretna (a town across the Mississippi from New Orleans), a beautiful, meticulously rendered two-storey mural marks the building that is home to the German American Cultural Center and Museum.

The museum, opened in 1999 with contributions from volunteers, traces the rich history and accomplishments of German immigrants in southern Louisiana.

The exhibits in the small museum are extremely well done, with many of the artifacts in almost mint condition. Displays depicting clothing, commerce, and industry tell the story of the immigrants' struggles and triumphs as they helped to build New Orleans and the surrounding area.

Two interesting exhibits tell of the more problematic aspects of ethnic assimilation in the early years of settlement, such as the practice of having surnames changed to sound more French: for example, Himmel became Hymel, Heidel became Haydel and Wishner became Vicknair. Many Orleanians may find out their roots are actually German as opposed to French.

Another exhibit highlights the trouble that those with German heritage and surnames faced during two world wars.

Starting in the early 18th century, Germans were lured to America by, among others, John Law, who perpetrated one of the biggest land frauds in history. Hardy Germans settled Des Allemands upriver from New Orleans on what is known as the *German Coast*. They helped supply the city with sustenance through farms and dairies after the great 1840 migration to America as Germans fled political upheaval. By 1860, New Orleans' population was one sixth German. In fact, the Faubourg Marigny had so many residents of German ancestry that it was called *Little Saxony*.

Even though by 1850 there were more Germans in New Orleans than French, the German contribution to the area has largely been overlooked by the general public: one of the missions of the museum is to raise awareness.

The center also has a genealogy facility with copious church records of births, deaths and marriages to help trace families back to Germany. The facilities, including Internet services, are free to the public.

The center has a hall for speakers and events on the first floor. The building and its surrounding property host year-round activities and are part of annual celebrations such as *Maifest* and *Oktoberfest*, which is incorporated into the annual Gretna Heritage Festival.

MEL OTT STATUE

Nice guys finish last

2301 Belle Chasse Highway
Tel: 504-363-1597
www.melottpark@gretnala.com
No near public transit

Mel Ott is the greatest baseball star ever to come out of the New Orleans area. He is honored in bronze with a life-size statue - depicting his signature high leg kick batting stance - outside Mel Ott Park, a baseball playground in his hometown of Gretna, a 10-minute ride from downtown New Orleans.

Ott's baseball journey began on the playing fields of Gretna, far away from New York and the famed *Polo Grounds*. After being rejected by the hometown Pelicans of the Southern Association, he was discovered by the great New York Giant manager John J. McGraw, who signed Ott to play for the Giants at the age of 17, beginning a 22-year Hall of Fame career. Ott would end his playing days as the career all-time home run leader of the National League with 511.

Ott is the only player from New Orleans to be enshrined in the *Baseball Hall of Fame* in Cooperstown, New York. At the time of his athletic feats, baseball was America's game. Every American boy knew Ott's name, making him a true immortal of the game.

When his playing career ended, Ott became the manager of the New York Giants. It is in that capacity that Ott entered into Bartlett's Quotations, playing a role in coining one of America's more famous bromides - "Nice guys finish last."

Here's what happened:

One day before a game between the Giants and cross-town rivals the Brooklyn Dodgers, sportswriters were giving the Dodgers' famously irascible skipper Leo Durocher a hard time for being such a testy personality. Durocher pointed over to his opponent and told reporters something to the effect of... "Look over there, that's Mel Ott, one of the nicest guys in the world, but where is he? Seventh place..." With some poetic and journalistic license, the saying morphed into the one we know today.

Ott, by all accounts, was a gentleman's gentleman. After moving back home to the New Orleans area he tragically died at the age of 49, the victim of a traffic accident on the Mississippi Gulf Coast.

Now, a beautiful life-size statue captures the fluid movement of Ott's homerun swing. And with his incredible records, Ott stands immortal, both in his hometown and in the minds of baseball fans everywhere.

Downtown

RACEHORSE GRAVES

A unique graveyard

1751 Gentilly Blvd.
Tel: 504-944-5515
www.fgno.com
Open: Every day 9.30am–12am
Free entry
#91 Jackson/Esplanade bus, #90 Carrolton bus or Canal Streetcar-City Park/
Museum

Although New Orleans is known for its above ground cemeteries, some of its most unusual graves can be found in an unexpected setting: the infield of the Fair Grounds Racetrack. A trio of small white markers signifies the resting place of three distinguished thoroughbred racehorses that captured the imagination of national and local racing fans.

Pan Zareta, named after the daughter of a mayor of Ciudad Juarez, Mexico, raced over 151 times in her career throughout the United States, Mexico and Canada, winning an amazing 76 times and finishing in the money in an almost unheard of 85 per cent of her races. She set or equaled 11 track records during her career and is known for setting a world record for five furlongs that stood for 31 years. Her accomplishments earned her the title "Queen of the Turf."

Black Gold, the winner of the 1924 Louisiana and Kentucky Derbies, is also interred in the infield. His career started at the Fair Grounds, where he won nine of 18 starts as a two-year-old. Black Gold went to win the 50th Kentucky Derby - notable as the first time the song *My Old Kentucky Home* was played before the race - in which he beat the establishment's "better bred" Kentucky horses.

That year by winning the Ohio and Chicago Derbies, Black Gold became the only thoroughbred to win derbies in four different states. On January 18, 1928, he broke his leg during a race at the Fair Grounds. Gamely, he finished the race on three legs even as his jockey tried to ease him up. A champion to the end, Black Gold was euthanized on the track and later buried along with Pan Zareta, ironically the only horse that his dam, U-See-it, never beat in a race.

Tenacious, winner of two consecutive New Orleans handicaps and a local star fondly remembered by old-timers. Although Tenacious actually died in Kentucky, the marker that is identical to Pan Zareta and Black God's grave markers, stands as a memorial.

The Fair Grounds Racetrack in the Gentilly section has been the site for horse racing since 1852 when it was home to the Union Racetrack (it has changed his names several times).

Horse racing at this site since 1852

1751 Gentilly Blvd.
Tel: 504-944-5515
www.fairgroundsracecourse.com
Open: 9am–12pm
#91 Esplanade/Jackson

T ucked away under the grandstand seating on the second floor of the Fair Grounds Racetrack is a timeline honoring and chronicling the men and women who contributed to the long and vivid history of horse racing at the venerable track.

The Fair Grounds Hall of Fame extends across the entire second floor in two sections. The glass cases displaying photos, artifacts and brief biographies of the inductees (both man and beast) are just steps away from the picture perfect paddock vistas provided by the newly constructed track; the old buildings were destroyed in a spectacular fire in 1993.

Saddles, vintage tack, riding silks of notable stables, beautiful silk programs, and photographs from back in the day all testify to racing's rich history in the Crescent City and the marriage of hard work and romance that typifies the Sport of Kings.

The timeline marks events in horse racing, both in America and at the 'Gentilly Oval', as the track is often referred to in the press.

The Fair Grounds - site of the New Orleans Jazz and Heritage Festival - has hosted horse racing since 1852, longer than the Fair Grounds meet which started in 1872 and is the third oldest thoroughbred track in the United States behind such storied tracks as Saratoga and Pimlico.

Members of the Hall include such American racing royalty as trainers Marion and Jack Van Berg, Hal Bishop and T.A. Grissom; jockeys Willie Shoemaker, Eddie Arcaro and Johnny Longden; owners Joe and Dorothy Brown, Louis Roussell III, Maggi Moss and Ben Jones; and notable horses such as Black Gold and Pan Zareta. Also included are local legends such as trainers Tom Amoss, Al Stall Jr., Frank Brothers, William Mott; horses Tenacious, Cabildo, No Le Hace, Risen Star; world renowned jockeys, including Eddie Delahoussaye, winner of two consecutive Kentucky Derbies, Craig Perret, Randy Romero and Robbie Albarado; personalities such as announcer John Kenneth "Jack" O'Hara, Allen "Black Cat" Lacombe; and General George Armstrong Custer of Little Big Horn fame (or infamy, depending on your outlook), who raced his horses at the 'Grounds.

The track itself served as a bivouac for U.S. Troops during World War I, but today you can partake of the Hall Of Fame and make your wager just footsteps away. And if you look around, you may just see a new generation of Hall Of Fame characters diligently trying to pick winners.

CREOLE CASTLE

A mysterious castle

View down the alley between 2424 and 2426 Aubry Street
#94 Broad Avenue bus

In almost complete anonymity, a mysterious castle, known only to a few Orleanians (mostly folks who live close to it), can be seen from a side street down an alley way between two modest New Orleans dwellings on Aubry Street. It is one of the true secrets of the city.

To find it you should travel down Rocheblave Street (pronounced Rush-Ah-Blave) to the end of the 1700 block then take a left on Aubry Street and travel four houses down. On the left, between the third and fourth houses, you'll clearly see the concrete turret and battlement. If you come by at night, the mystery is given more heft by a light shining in the small window of the turret.

In the book *Creoles of New Orleans*, published in 1987 by Lyla Hay Owen and Owen Murphy, the castle is called the Creole Castle for its geographical location situated in the Seventh Ward, the heartland of New Orleans Creole culture. The area is renowned, among other things, for its craftsmen: bricklayers, carpenters and plasterers - the backbone of New Orleans' African American middle class.

According to interviews conducted by the authors, the castle was built circa 1921 by an Austrian gentleman named Rudolpho.

Ms. Emily Trevigne, whose family lived next door, remembers Rudolpho building the castle piece by piece with the help of a local man. Trevigne is quoted as saying that Rudolpho built his castle over her family's property line and that her father complained. She also claims that her father, contrary to Rudolpho's protestations, was proved right, as Rudolpho had to pay a monetary settlement for building beyond the line. She remembers the castle being so close to her home that she could reach out and almost touch its bathtub.

Neighbors on Aubry Street also tell a romantic story that may explain the existence of this mysterious dwelling: the builder of the castle, possibly Rudolpho, met a woman in Italy and fell in love. The lady lived in a castle and told her new love she would only follow him to New Orleans if he built her a castle.

LE MUSÉE DE F.P.C.

A collection that illuminates the struggle of a vibrant community

2336 Esplanade Avenue
Tel: 504-233-0384
www.lemuseedefpc.com
Open: Tue–Sat 11am–4pm, Sunday 1pm–4pm. Tours available Wed–Sun at 1pm by appointment
Entry fee: $15
#91 Jackson/Esplanade bus

Opened in 2009 and housed in a beautifully maintained and restored Greek Revival residence on Esplanade Avenue, Le Musée de f.p.c (museum of New Orleans' free people of color) is a perfect primer in a gracious setting that explains things that many history books either gloss over or fail to adequately examine. To anyone who wishes to understand the laws and social conditions affecting a people who, despite a pre-Civil War 80 per cent literacy rate, could not vote or even shop at stores, the museum and its compelling narrative will not disappoint. Each room of the elegant mansion is appointed with period furnishings, paintings, pictures, drawings and photos of prominent free people of color who lived the tale expertly woven here by docents. Most of the exhibits are from the collection of founders Drs. Dwight and Beverly McKenna, who spent years gathering materials they wished to one day share with the public.

The collection's focus on the achievements of free people of color illuminates the struggle of the vibrant community in New Orleans that once made up a third of the city's population. Notables such as Marie Laveau, the scientist Norbert Rillieux, and Homer Plessy (of Plessy v. Ferguson fame) number among them.

One lesser-known figure to the outside world (and even to many Orleanians) gets a star turn here and deservedly so: Dr. Louis Charles Roudanez, to whom the museum is dedicated, was a surgeon and activist who published two newspapers in the Civil War era. Educated in France (as were many free people of color in the 19th century), he was a successful man of African and French descent, but he was not allowed to vote or hold public office.

The stories told here are of an ever-changing universe of laws and handicaps constantly preventing these citizens from fully participating in the civic and social life of their times. It is a complicated narrative, as many free people of color had property (including slaves in some cases) and had paid millions of dollars of property taxes in the decades leading up to the Civil War, prospering under the economic system that was based on slavery. As many as 3000 community members volunteered to serve in the Confederate army at the outbreak of the war.

Free people of color

In the history of slavery in the Americas, the term 'free people of color' at first specifically referred to persons of mixed African and European descent who were not slaves. The term was especially used in the French colonies, including Louisiana, and settlements on Caribbean islands, such as Saint-Domingue (Haiti), Guadeloupe, and Martinique.

GENERAL LAUNDRY BUILDING ⑤

Vibrant colors speaking through decades loud and clear

2512 St. Peter Street
#94 Broad bus

Tucked down a side street less than a block away from a refurbished public housing project on the border of Treme, the crumbling Art Deco façade of the General Laundry building harkens back to what was once considered the cutting edge of modernity; its vibrant yellows, blues, greens and oranges speaking through the decades loud and clear.

Geometric shapes, fluted columns, terracotta floral motifs and zig-zags – all trademarks of the Art Deco architecture of the 1930s – still shine through the ferns, weeds and vines growing through cracks in the gorgeous artwork.

Once upon a time, the building was a showcase of urban design and was even included in a 1974 retrospective at Finch College celebrating Art Deco architecture and specimens of the era. The General Laundry found itself in good company in the exhibition alongside more well-known structures such as the Waldorf Astoria, Rockefeller Center and the Chrysler Building.

Robert Chapoit, proprietor of General Laundry, built this beauti-ful building after a fire destroyed the former home of the business. It is believed that Chapoit had a hand in the design. The new building opened to much fanfare in 1930 with a party that included free food, an orchestra and dancing that continued well into the night

Today, sadness emanates from the shabby, neglected condition of the property. Indeed, it seems to be living on borrowed time, already dodging the wrecking ball not once, but twice.

The U. S. Postal Service purchased the property in 1974 with an eye to razing it and using it as a parking lot. Preservationists moved in and through their efforts the building was listed on the National Register of Historic Places, saving the structure.

The latest owner is a salvage company looking to knock it down and expand the footprint of their neighbouring business. However, the com-pany had to clear those plans with the State His-toric Preservation Office and new governmental protocols prevented the building from coming down. The future of the historic beauty still seems tenuous at best. Today it sits as if waiting for some-thing or someone to come along and save it.

BANKSY GRAFFITI: "UMBRELLA GIRL"

Almost stolen in 2014

Corner of Kerlerec and North Rampart Streets
#5 Marigny-Bywater bus, # 88 St Claude-Jackson Barracks bus,
#91 Jackson-Esplanade bus

A block from the French Quarter in the Faubourg Marigny, a beautiful piece of graffiti on a wall shows a young girl standing under her umbrella. Rain falls on the girl from inside the umbrella. The graffiti is protected by a clear Plexiglas sheet.

This artwork is believed to be the work of the international guerilla artist Banksy, who is said to have swooped into New Orleans to paint 14 satirical works on public walls throughout the city in 2008. Of the three that now remain, "Umbrella Girl" is the most prominent. In an interview Banksy explained that the image represented how things that are supposed to protect us can also hurt us.

Another of the remaining artworks is at the corner of Clio and Carondelet, while the third and perhaps most stealthily placed is behind an old fire station on Jackson Avenue near the river.

According to one art writer, many Orleanians welcomed Banksy's ghostlike presence with the same excitement reserved for another English import, the Beatles, who played at New Orleans City Park in 1964. The hunt (or art watch, as it were) was then on.

Once bestowed upon New Orleans and left to fend for herself, "Umbrella Girl" was subjected to an all too familiar aspect of urban life. She was almost the victim of a crime. As Banksy's work has fetched prices at auction of over a million dollars, the pilfering of his work from the public walls that serve as his canvas is not uncommon.

In February 2014, neighbors noticed a man trying to chisel the art off the wall in broad daylight. The man claimed to be an art removal expert working on behalf of the property owner, with the goal of bringing "Umbrella Girl" to the Tate Museum in London.

After a local photographer took a picture of the man, calls to authorities and vigilance by members of the neighborhood frightened off the would-be thief. He jumped into his rental van and got away, but without the painting. He was later identified as an art dealer from Los Angeles.

"HANK WAS HERE 1955" ETCHING

An urban literary hieroglyph

1431 Royal Street in front of R Bar
Tel: 504 -948-7499
www.royalstreetinn.com
#5 Marigny-Bywater bus or Riverfront streetcar

Scrawled in the concrete in the sidewalk in front of a bar in the Faubourg Marigny section of the city, various etchings have been left for posterity by unknown souls. If you take the time to look closely, one of the imprints surrounded by a crude heart shape states, "HANK WAS HERE 1955".

This inscription is believed to be the work of Charles Bukowski, whose proper name was Henry Charles Bukowski. Those closest to him called him Hank. Indeed, the proprietors of the bar have rooms upstairs for rent and for a time had a room named after Bukowksi, to honor the urban hieroglyph sitting outside.

Bukowski and New Orleans, with its drinking and horse racing pedigree, seem to have been made for each other. On his first trip east from his home in Los Angeles in 1942 to explore the world, one of his main destinations was the Crescent City.

He worked in New Orleans as an errand boy for the *New Orleans Item*, a daily newspaper that, interestingly enough, was a paper that William Faulkner and Lafcadio Hearn also worked for when they first came to the city.

It was during World War II that Bukowski called New Orleans home. After receiving a draft notice from the New Orleans draft board, he sent them a letter informing them he would not be reporting due to his "personal philosophy." The board threatened to turn him in to the authorities so he showed up and was rejected, before being called back for re-evaluation in 1943. He was tracked down in Philadelphia later that year and incarcerated in a Pennsylvania prison for 17 days, before again being rejected for medical reasons.

Over the years, Bukowski was said to have traveled to New Orleans on many occasions. It was here that he gained the impetus that catapulted him into the literary consciousness of the world: the well-regarded Loujon Press brought Bukowski back to New Orleans in the early 60s and published his first two books of poetry: *It Catches My Heart in Its Hands* and *Crucifix in a Death Hand.*

The publishers of Loujon (Jon and Gypsy Lou Webb) had a deal with Bukowski: they would advance him money to go to the track and

he would write them a book of poetry. Day after day he would take his stipend to the track without producing the promised manuscript. When the Webbs balked at handing over his gambling money, he sat down and wrote a manuscript in less than two days. He was back at the track and on his way to literary history.

SAINT ROCH CHAPEL

The patron saint of miraculous cures

1725 St. Roch Avenue
Tel: 504-596-3050
www.arch-no.org
Open: Mon–Sat 9am–3pm, Sunday 9am–12pm
#80 Desire-Louisa bus

The high-vaulted, blue-ceilinged chapel of the National Shrine of St. Roch (the patron saint of miraculous cures) was built in 1875 by the Reverend P. L. Thevis, a German immigrant, in order to fulfill a promise.

Today, a tiny room stage left from the altar, no larger than a broom closet, is filled with flowers, crutches, toys, glass eyes, braces and prosthetics of all kinds as a tribute to cures and hopes of future cures.

On days when the chapel is closed, a window on the right side at the back of the chapel allows visitors to peer in and see the displays of grateful piety.

Yellow fever was a major cause of death when Father Thevis arrived in New Orleans, so he made a vow that if none of his parishioners perished from "Bronze John," as as the virus was poetically nicknamed, he would build a chapel to thank and honor St. Roch.

Against all odds, none of his parishioners died as a result of the fever. The "miracle" did not go unnoticed and the chapel soon became a destination for those in need of healing.

The afflicted brought offerings to St. Roch. Many left plaster feet, arms, hearts and crutches, and soon the anteroom to the right of the chapel altar became a depository for these tokens of hope and gratitude.

Entering the cemetery from St. Roch Avenue, the gates are flanked by two curious angel figures whose wings are now long gone, blown away by a hurricane years ago.

The walkway leads from the gate toward the chapel through two neat rows of New Orleans-style above ground tombs. The cemetery has many more tombs and many coping graves (small family plots surrounded by short walls filled in with soil or marble chips).

Assistance in finding a husband

There are also large statues of the Stations of the Cross at intervals around the perimeter of the cemetery walls in between the walls of mausoleums. The cemetery is the site of a traditional Stations of the Cross devotion on Good Friday; legend has it that single women who come on that day to ask for St. Roch's assistance in finding a husband will be successful.

JESSICA'S GARDEN

A beautiful anomaly

Corner of St. Claude Avenue and Montegut Street on the neutral ground
Open: 24 hours daily
#88 St. Claude/Jackson Barracks bus

When the inevitable traffic backup occurs at the corner of St. Claude Avenue and Montegut Street, less than a block away from the railroad crossing where the Bywater neighborhood begins, motorists can often be seen rolling down their windows to ask the volunteers about the garden they're tending.

Jessica's Garden was conceived and maintained by Jessica Hawk's former fiancée and friend Lee Horvitz after Ms. Hawk's untimely death in 2008. This beautiful anomaly on a well-traveled inner city thoroughfare was built to last a hundred years, yet as commuters pour by the neutral ground, most are unaware of the significance of Jessica's Garden, now meticulously tended as a tribute to love and friendship.

Jessica and Lee moved to New Orleans together in 2003 and had plans to marry. They called off the wedding but remained good friends until the shocking events of Ms. Hawk's brutal murder in her apartment close to where the garden stands today. The postgraduate's murder went unsolved until 2014 when police announced the break in the case that led to the crime being solved.

Mr. Horvitz started an awareness campaign called 'Justice for Jessica'. At the suggestion of local horticulturist Harold Applewhite, he built the garden that is now supported by an online fund and maintained by friends of Jessica.

Ms. Hawk, who received the first post-Katrina scholarship from the University of New Orleans, was a botanist, so a garden seemed a fitting memorial. It consists of several raised flower and herb beds that include some of Jessica's favorites. A tree stands in the middle of the garden and there are benches for visitors to sit and contemplate as traffic whizzes by on St. Claude.

There are plaques with some of Jessica's favorite quotes (including one by Tennessee Williams); a concrete slab where Jessica's friends and loved ones signed their names in paint after a second line parade in Jessica's honor at the garden dedication in 2012; and a brick platform beneath one of the benches that evokes the nature of Jessica's life. The subjects imprinted on the bricks include Shakespeare, Vivaldi, David Bowie, Billie Holliday, Botany, Woody Allen, Monty Python and Ernie K. Doe, giving a rich flavor of a curious life ended too soon.

ROSALIE ALLEY

A portal to the voodoo afterworld?

Middle of the 3300 block of N. Rampart between Piety and Desire
#88 St Claude/Jackson Barracks bus or #5 Marigny/Bywater bus

In the Bywater section of New Orleans, in the middle of North Rampart Street between Piety and Desire, Rosalie Alley is a half block long gravel alleyway with a quiet residential vibe by day. Yet from the moment you pass the cartoon-like metal sculpture of a Ghede (skeleton) on the sidewalk from N. Rampart, it's evident you're not in just any old alleyway.

A few feet into the alley is a makeshift brick fountain with a small ceramic skull. The fountain is backed by a very large mural depicting famed voodoo priestess Marie Laveau.

As you continue deeper into the alley you are greeted by a small army of Ghedes painted on either side on the wooden fences. Ghedes are spiritual figures in voodoo that represent wise men who have accumulated all the knowledge of the dead. They stand at the center of all roads that lead to the afterworld.

The Ghedes found in Rosalie Alley don't seem menacing; many of them have expressions that border on joyful, if not blatantly playful. One of the more prominent Ghedes sports a big smile and a cigar.

The pathway that leads down Rosalie Alley has front doors, back yards and even what appears to be a communal patio with a chessboard, chairs, tables and bathtubs filled with thriving plants that give the small area a lived-in feel.

The pastel-colored fences, further decorated with slogans written in French and Spanish, also lend a Caribbean flavor to this unusual urban pocket.

The art in Rosalie Alley is the work of Voodoo priestess Sallie Ann Glassman, who every July presides at the Hurricane Protection Spell (a mixture of Catholic ritual and Voodoo ceremony) in the hope of warding off the tropical storms that bedevil New Orleans' well-being.

Believers gather for the ceremony further down the 250-foot-long alleyway at Achade Meadow Peristyle to leave offerings to Our Lady of Prompt Succor and to the voodoo figure Ezil Danto. The offerings to Our Lady include flowers, statues, candles, religious pictures, while the gifts for Ezil Danto cater to his tastes, which include rum, Florida water, daggers, unfiltered cigarettes, fried pork and king cakes.

Some say that there is even more to Rosalie Alley; they believe the symbol-rich fences lead to the legendary portals of the afterworld, the Gates of Guinee. According to these believers, it is unwise for anyone to visit the alley alone lest they be pulled into the afterworld from which there is no escape.

THE VICTORY ARCH

⑪

First memorial built to honor soldiers of the Great War

3801-3899 Burgundy Street
#88 St Claude bus, #5 Marigny/Bywater bus

Erected in 1919 by the people of the Ninth Ward of New Orleans, Victory Arch was the first memorial of its kind, honoring citizens who enlisted to fight in the Great War as well as those who lost their lives in the conflict.

Located in the historic Bywater neighborhood, the memorial is built in the style of a Roman triumphal arch. The monument, known more formally as the Ninth Ward Memorial Arch, was constructed with money raised entirely in the working class neighborhood through house-to-house canvassing, personal subscriptions and fundraisers.

Measuring 28.6 feet high, 21.2 feet wide and seven feet thick, the monument was designed by renowned monument artist Charles L. Lawhon, who was famed for his designs of many tombs in New Orleans' famous above-ground cemeteries.

On it, four cast bronze plaques list the names of all residents of the Ninth Ward who served in combat or were killed in action, along with those who later died from their wounds. Both black and white citizens are listed there, indicating the biracial nature of many old New Orleans neighborhoods.

The names show the ethnic mix of the neighborhood: French, Irish, German, English, Scottish, Spanish, and Croatian surnames abound, many still familiar to lifelong New Orleanians. Their descendants (politicians, musicians, jurists, artists, physicians, attorneys and business people who are our friends and neighbors today) enjoy the fruits of the sacrifices made by these citizen soldiers.

There are 1,231 men and women memorialized on the monument. Frances Ruth Fabing, a combat nurse for the Red Cross during the war and the only woman honored, was called on to unveil the arch at the 1919 dedication. The arch stands at the edge of what was known as McArty Square facing Burgundy Street (pronounced 'bur-GUN-dee' in the New Orleanian way), just outside the backyard of KIPP Reniassance High School.

It is somewhat ironic that the first memorial to World War I was funded by the deeply patriotic community of New Orleans' Ninth Ward, yet nearly a century later, after Hurricane Katrina knocked down the levees that protected the neighborhood, many questioned the value of New Orleans as an American city. Perhaps this demonstrates the value of remembering history.

They eat anything that doesn't eat them first

4511 St. Claude Avenue
Tel: 504-292-7831 (call for opening hours)
#5 Marigny-Bywater bus or #88 St. Claude-Jackson Barracks bus

igh on a pole, so it can be seen from the bridge as it crosses the Industrial Canal, a sign reads "COWAN MAN."

On the street that sits a storey lower than the bridge approach, necessitating the tall sign, is a neat painted wooden house where the exotic protein of the outer reaches of the Louisiana culinary landscape can be found for human consumption.

Some of the out of the ordinary fare to be found here includes Cowan (snapping turtles), alligator meat, garfish, muskrats and, as the almost cult-like flier proclaims "Coons, Coons Coons!" - raccoon being quite a delicacy to some in these parts.

There are, of course, the old jokes about the tendency of the Cajuns of Louisiana being known to basically eat anything that doesn't eat them first. Here is a place that puts the meat into that story front and center.

The proprietor of this colorful enterprise, who introduces himself as Seafood Frank, has been at it since 1959. When he's not tending to his trade, sporting a large apron, he can be found on his Facebook page advertising familiar Louisiana seafood staples such as soft-shell crabs, jumbo shrimp, catfish filets and trout filets.

What makes the place noteworthy, however, is the more colorful fare on offer, such as venison and alligator sausage, whole cleaned rabbits, possum, whole wild pigs and large goats, along with the reptilian delights of alligator and snapping turtle. Whole skinned alligator, flayed and wrapped up ready to be barbequed, and live snapping turtles fresh enough that they can "take your finger right off" can be cleaned while you wait. And as for the "Coons! Coons! Coons!" advertised on the Xeroxed black and white menu advertisements, one may ask, "How do you prepare that, anyway?"

In a magazine article a few years ago, Ronald Lewis, curator of the House of Dance and Feathers, is quoted praising the succulence of this dish and describing how his mother used to prepare raccoon. According to Lewis, she would boil it in seafood boil then bake it with sweet potatoes. With the certainty of someone who knows of what he speaks he added, "That's good".

MUSIC BOX VILLAGE

A magical place

4557 N. Rampart Street
www.musicboxvillage.com
#5 Marigny- Bywater bus or #88 St. Claude-Jackson Barracks bus

In the midst of a densely populated and weathered urban environment, hidden from view by a corrugated metal wall with steel beams protruding in a crown-like manner, Airlift Music Box is the permanent home of one of the more unique examples of New Orleans' passion for music and architecture.

A collection of structures built to be musical instruments, the place is made out of found materials such as abandoned lumber, windows, ropes, fans, paint cans, chimes, cannibalized light fixtures and every sort of building material imaginable.

This sylvan plot with a generous sprinkling of trees is a magical place within spitting distance of the Industrial Canal bisecting New Orleans Ninth Ward, today home to a thriving community of artists and artisans.

Having begun in 2011, the Music Box village was set the following year in a secret location in New Orleans' City Park, only blocks from the Jazz and Heritage Festival; it hosted musicians who were appearing at that year's Fest. It popped up again in City Park for a short lived incarnation in 2015, leading to this artistic vision becoming reality in its new home in the fall of 2016.

The vision is as ambitious as it is creative, looking toward a future when it will be home not only to musical performances, but also artist residencies, educational summer camps for kids, concerts and, of course, the ever-changing collection of instruments: the Chateau Poulet - a structure that looks like a witch's hat incorporating rope-activated fans to produce different tones: the large lace bell that is home to an assortment of smaller bells; and other structures designed to produce sound by walking on calibrated boards that create music as weight is shifted across them.

Part of the new property includes a metal fabrication business and workshop equipped with massive cranes, welding equipment, hole punchers and an array of tools to facilitate the construction of future architectural instruments as yet unimagined. Eventually, the space will also contain the Swamp Dityrambalina - a full-scale musical house that made its debut in an earlier incarnation of the Music Box.

In the future, organizers of the Music Box village hope to lure every kind of musician, from children (peepholes have been included in the metal wall for kids to look in even if they cannot afford to enter) to world-famous artists in an effort not only to be inclusive, but also to encourage what the founders call "genre-bending" artists.

A new musical experiment in New Orleans is born.

DOULLUT STEAMBOAT HOUSES

Houses built to resemble riverboats

400 and 503 Egania Street
Private residences not open to the public
#88 St. Claude/Jackson Barracks bus
for security reasons a car or taxi is recommended

I f you find yourself walking in the Holy Cross section of the Lower Nine, very near the Mississippi River levee, you may see two mansions on Egania Street that appear to be inspired by wedding cakes. These are known as the steamboat houses and were built to resemble Mississipi riverboats by a husband and wife team of river pilots Milton and Mary Doullhutt. The houses are now privately owned and not open to the public, so they can only be admired from the outside. But to those in the know and from stories in the press, the interiors are just as interesting and have many architectural similarities to the riverboats that the Doullut family enjoyed.

Decks encircle the houses, forming porches that are draped with strands of huge cypress balls like a giant pearl necklace. Metal smokestacks in place of chimneys, woodwork reflecting the steamboat era and of course the top floors that bring to mind open pilot houses with a commanding view of the river are some of the obvious exterior features of what are widely known as the 'Steamboat Houses'.

The opulent style of the riverboat continues indoors, with narrow halls and steep staircases, walls and ceilings covered in pressed zinc panels, their cornstalk and cross hatched patterns resembling a kind of three-dimensional wall paper. Oval stained glass windows reminiscent of portholes add another maritime touch. The houses were built on the highest land in the neighborhood, enabling them to survive the floodwaters of Katrina, which devastated much of the newer surrounding properties.

In 1905, river pilots Milton and Mary Doullut built the first of two houses to resemble the riverboats that they had guided up and down the river in their professional capacity. Eight years later, the Doulluts built for their son another steamboat house close to the first. Further evidence that Orleanians once had a firmer grasp of geographic imperatives as applied to home construction is the fact that the entire bottom floors of both houses are coated inside and out with ceramic tiles, meaning that each house can literally be hosed out after a flood. Even the upright columns that support the wrap around porch are sheathed in white tile castings.

New Orleans being New Orleans and in possession of a contrary streak, there always seems to be more. Architects who have studied the Steamboat Houses also point out that the pagoda inspired roof design and tiles were most probably patterned after the Japanese exhibit at the 1904 World's Fair in St Louis. That's New Orleans - uniqueness stacked upon uniqueness.

The Doullut Steamboat Houses at 400 and 503 Egania Street were designated as historical landmarks in 1977.

HOUSE OF DANCE
AND FEATHERS

New Orleans celebratory street culture

1317 Tupelo Street
Tel: 504-957-2678 for appointments
www.houseofdanceandfeathers.org
#88 St. Claude/Jackson Barracks bus

In a large shed in a Lower Ninth Ward backyard, a real feast of colorful expressions of New Orleans' African American celebratory street culture is waiting to be explored. The small room is crammed from floor to ceiling with stuff. Mardi Gras Indian costumes with elaborate beading, appliqué and feathers catch the eye immediately. They are joined here by a veritable sea of manmade artifacts: a mosaic is formed from street signage; there are music posters and Second Line umbrellas, masks, photos and books. It can be overwhelming to those unprepared for it all, but the genial and enthusiastic host, Ronald W. Lewis, is almost always on hand, happy to share his knowledge of his beloved culture with the world.

Lewis has been accumulating memorabilia based around the urban street celebrations of New Orleans for years. He came home one day to find his wife, weary of the clutter, had put his "things" into the backyard. Soon the House of Dance and Feathers was on its way to becoming the vibrant attraction it is today.

Denied entry into the social fabric of white society in New Orleans, the African American population invented their own traditions, such as Second Lines, where spectators of a parade join in by following the procession. Social Aid and Pleasure Clubs were formed to provide medical assistance and funeral services to the disenfranchised black community, and also to provide social outlets, which have since manifested into long-standing organizations such as Zulu, the premier African American Mardi Gras parade.

Lewis can also explain the genesis of some of New Orleans' lesser-known African American street phenomena, such as the Baby Dolls, which started in 1912 in the red light districts as a reaction to Jim Crow's laws. It was also a way for African American women to join in the fun and subtle subversion of Carnival, a tradition that has been revived in recent years. The Northside Skull and Bones Gang is another of New Orleans' oldest Mardi Gras traditions dating back to 1819.

At the end of your visit you'll no doubt agree with the slogan that Ronald Lewis has for guests: "Come in a stranger, leave a friend!"

KATRINA GRAFFITI

(16)

An exaggerated sign to deter looters

Ansel Stroud Jr. Military Museum
6400 St. Claude Avenue
Tel: 504-278-8664
www.geauxguardmuseums.org
Open: Mon–Sat 10am–4pm
Free entry
#88 St. Claude-Jackson Barracks bus

"Don't [*sic*] try. I am sleeping inside with a big dog an ugli woman two shotguns and a claw hammer".

One of the iconic images of Hurricane Katrina, this famous graffiti graced the outside of an oriental rug business on St. Charles Avenue in the chaotic days right after the storm.

Although most Orleanians probably won't know it, this sign, along with numerous other specimens of graffiti that were photographed after the tragedy and sent to worldwide media, now resides in the Ansel Stroud Jr. Military Museum at Jackson Barracks.

The signs were the work of Bob Rue, a rug merchant, whose message of guns, dog, ugly woman and hammer were exaggerated for effect in an attempt to deter would-be looters. Rue admits he spent most of the time after Katrina at his girlfriend's house, high and dry in Uptown New Orleans, although he does claim that he did in fact have a claw hammer.

But his signs became a media magnet that garnered Mr. Rue visits from American media stars such as Tim Russert, Anderson Cooper and Geraldo Rivera, who stopped by to get the story.

Rue's signs were eventually sold to the State of Louisiana and since the storm have spent time displayed in other museums, such as the Presbytyre in New Orleans and the Newseum in Washington, D.C. One of the plywood panels is now even stored at the Smithsonian.

And what is perhaps the world's most famous claw hammer can even be found in a glass case just to the left of the signs.

ANSEL M. STROUD JR. MILITARY HISTORY & WEAPONS MUSEUM

U.S. Grant, Robert E. Lee, P.G.T. Beauregard and Zachary Taylor were all stationed here

6400 St. Claude Avenue
Tel: 504-278-8664
www.geauxguardmuseums.com
Open: Mon–Sat 10am–4pm
#88 St. Claude/Jackson Barracks bus

In the middle of historic Jackson Barracks National Guard base, surrounded by warplanes and a dozen or so military vehicles, the Ansel M. Stroud Jr. Military History & Weapons Museum is dedicated to collecting, preserving and interpreting the distinguished history of the Louisiana Army and Air National Guard.

Completely refurbished after being devastated by Hurricane Katrina, the facility is now a gleaming repository that spans the entire history of the United States military in Louisiana.

Exhibits explain contributions of the Guard through text, paintings, photos and an extensive collection of military hardware, including Revolutionary era muskets, mortars, handguns, rifles, cannons, small tanks, airplane cockpits, missiles, a helicopter and captured enemy ordinance.

Memorabilia dates from before statehood all the way up to the destruction and rebirth of Jackson Barracks, with videos of that event featuring eyewitness accounts from the Guardsmen who experienced it and served the community so valiantly.

The base was established in 1834 as a result of the Federal Fortifications Act of 1832. At that time, the United States government determined that coastal areas of the new country were not adequately defended. Jackson Barracks, then named New Orleans Barracks (along with Fort Pike and Fort McComb) was built to protect the lower Mississippi River.

Jackson Barracks' first major war was the Mexican War (1846-1848). U.S. Grant, Robert E. Lee, Zachary Taylor and P.G.T. Beauregard were all stationed at the base, although not at the same time. During this time, the Public Service Hospital for Veterans was built, thereby becoming the first veterans' hospital in United States history. The hospital was torn down in 1888.

It was here in 1920 that General Pershing reviewed troops returning from the fighting in World War I. The 39th and 40th regiments of African-American troops were consolidated into the 25th regiment, becoming famous as the Buffalo Soldiers who fought in the Indian wars and the Spanish American War, adding to the significant military history associated with Jackson Barracks.

The base was renamed in 1866 for President Andrew Jackson, who famously led American forces to victory at the Battle of New Orleans in the War of 1812 at Chalmette Battlefield about a mile away.

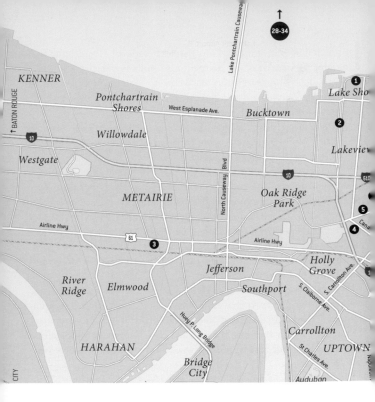

Lake Area

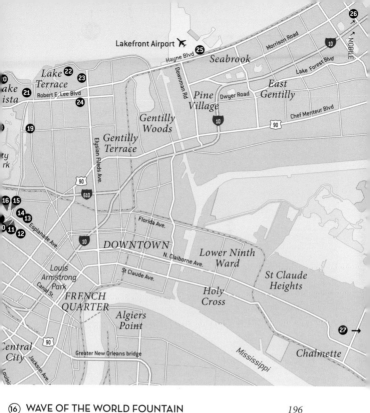

MARDI GRAS FOUNTAIN

Crests of all the city's carnival krewes

Lakeshore Drive
Nearest bus connection #45 Lakeview (approx. 7 to 10 blocks away)

Dedicated on September 16, 1962, the Mardi Gras Fountain added some excitement to the New Orleans lakefront.

The fountain is ringed by large ceramic plates displaying the crests of all of the city's carnival krewes (private social clubs that put on the balls and parades that make up the bulk of New Orleans Mardi Gras events).

New Orleans lakefront is a surprisingly quiet section of the city. A few sailboats, the occasional jogger and perhaps a lone fisherman are often all that can be found on the south bank of Lake Pontchartrain, the 10th largest lake in the United States. But despite well-tended grass and picnic tables, it is almost devoid of what could be called attractions.

Enter New Orleans Mardi Gras. In the 1950s, Darwin Fenner, the leader of the elite Rex carnival krewe, sent his young float designer Blaine Kern on a tour of Europe for inspiration. Kern, now a world-renowned float builder, was impressed with the fountains that grace the grand cities of Europe. Upon his return home he approached Gerald Gallinghouse, then president of the New Orleans Levee Board, with an idea to build a fountain on the lakefront to honor the city's carnival krewes. Thus, the Mardi Gras Fountain was born.

During the 60s and 70s the fountain was very popular, shooting up at intervals 30-foot pulsing streams of water illuminated by lights of purple, green and gold, the official colors of Mardi Gras. But New Orleans seems to have a penchant for creating ruins out of its newer monuments and by the 90s, the fountain was a stagnant remnant of itself.

One tradition that grew around the new fountain was to fill the its pool with laundry detergent, an adolescent mischief that probably contributed to the site falling into disrepair.

In 2005 the city started a $2.5 million refurbishing of the fountain, including new sidewalks and enhanced mechanical systems. Kern's artists added more plaques for krewes that did not exist in 1962 as well as repairing or replacing some original ceramic plates that had been damaged. All of this was completed just in time for Hurricane Katrina.

In 2013 another renovation began with the help of FEMA and the Army Corps of Engineers. And a new security system was installed, no doubt to fend off soap-wielding terrorists.

CELTIC CROSS

A testament to thousands of Irish immigrants

West End Blvd. and Down Street on the neutral ground
Open: 24 hours daily
#45 Lakeview bus or Canal–Cemeteries streetcar then transfer to #45 Lakeview bus

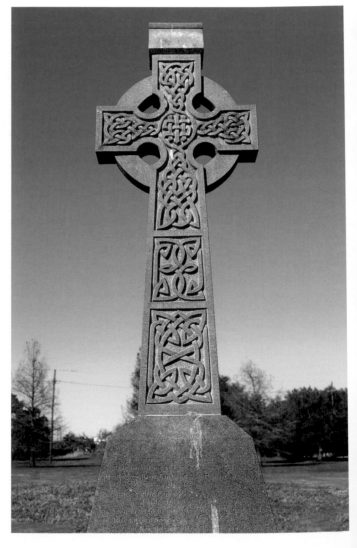

F rom hallowed ground in the middle of the prosperous middle class neighborhood of Lakeview, a lone Kilkenny marble cross looks out into the vast New Orleans neutral ground of West End Boulevard, upon hallowed ground in the middle of the prosperous middle class neighborhood of Lakeview. It stands as, a testament to the thousands of Irish immigrants who built the New Basin Canal at great cost in suffering and lives.

The site of the Celtic cross at the West End has recently been expanded to include a four-acre interpretive park provided by the Ancient Order of the Hibernians to celebrate and commemorate the vast and lasting contributions of the Irish community to the culture and history of New Orleans.

The memorial was dedicated in 1990 by the Irish Cultural Society of New Orleans, and the ceremony was attended by the Irish ambassador to the United States to honor the sacrifice of the men who excavated arguably the greatest public works project of 19th-century New Orleans.

The canal was started in 1832 and it took six years to build the shipping channel route that was meant to compete with the Carondelet Canal, a major portal for trade between Lake Pontchartrain and the Creole section of the city. The New Basin Canal would connect the lake to the Faubourg St. Mary (which today now is the Central Business District), and was conceived to take advantage of the booming economy of the American sector, which was emerging as the financial powerhouse of the city. Schooners brought produce, lumber, bricks and commodities of all kinds that tied New Orleans into the economy of the entire region. The canal was in fact a tremendous financial success and contributed to the flourishing growth of the city's economy for almost a hundred years. The canal was filled in after World War II, and its route was incorporated in the building of the Pontchartrain Expressway in the 1960s, which is now part of the U.S. Interstate Highway System.

Thousands of Irish immigrants dug through an unforgiving cypress swamp to create the canal. Slave labor, readily available at the time, was not utilized because of the dangerous working conditions; , for the slaves' lives were deemed more valuable than that the lives of immigrant laborers. Yellow fever, cholera and malaria, along with brutal working conditions, claimed anywhere from 6,000 to 30,000 lives of workers from the Emerald Isle -, and all for the wage of one dollar a day.

Such were the conditions that many died where they stood and were buried in the levees of the canal or in the mud and shells of the roadways where they fell. Thousands were given neither last rites nor grave markers.

GRAM PARSONS' GRAVE

A kidnapped corpse

Garden of Memories Cemetery
4900 Airline Drive
Tel: 504-833-3786
www.gardenofmemoriesmetairie.com
Open: 24 hours daily
#E2 bus

GRAM PARSONS
Nov. 7, 1946-Sept. 19, 1973

Another young man safely strummed,
his silver string guitar
And he played to people everywhere
Some say he was a star
But he was just a country boy,
His simple songs confess
And the music he had in him,
So very few possess.
From "In My Hour Of Darkness"

Your soul lives on through your music.
Your spirit lives on in our hearts.

A bronze funerary tablet rests in the meticulously landscaped sub-urban cemetery just outside New Orleans. It seems incongruous, given that the young man depicted on the slab, singing and playing his guitar, is a musician closely associated with the rock culture of the 60s and 70s rather than with New Orleans music.

The tombstone marks the final resting place of the remains of Gram Parsons, considered one of the greatest rock artists of his generation. Parsons was a successful member of such important bands as The Byrds, The Flying Burrito Brothers and many others of that era.

Born in Florida, Parsons is said to have been inspired to become a musician when at the age of nine he saw Elvis perform live. He was named the 87th most influential rock musician in a Rolling Stone top 100 poll in 2003. He was also honored for his blending of genres and is given credit for helping to create the 'country rock' and 'alt country' genres.

But with no obvious links to New Orleans, the curious may wonder: why here? The story does not disappoint.

Right before his death at the age of 26, Parsons made a pact with his band mates that in the event of his demise, he wished to be cremated and his remains buried at the Joshua Tree Monument. Shortly after his wishes were expressed, he met an untimely end due to a reported over-dose of morphine and tequila.

Parsons' stepfather, who is believed to have lived in Metairie (a sub-urb of New Orleans) at the time, immediately made plans to have his stepson's body brought back to Metairie for burial. However, Parsons' friends had other ideas. While the body was being prepared for travel to Louisiana, they rented a hearse, kidnapped the body at LAX airport in California and drove it to the Joshua Tree Monument. Once in the desert, they splashed gasoline on the body in the open casket and set it on fire.

Seeing headlights, presumably those of the authorities moving in their direction, the body snatchers skedaddled, leaving the burning corpse behind. The authorities dowsed the fire and the remaining 60% of Gram Parsons' body was sent to the suburban New Orleans cemetery, were it lies in rest today.

KATRINA MEMORIAL AND MAUSOLEUM TO UNCLAIMED BODIES

Perhaps the least known of the Katrina memorials

5050 Canal Street
Tel: 225-342-9500
www.saveourcemeteries.org/charity-hospital
Open: hours vary
Canal–Cemeteries streetcar

Nestled between two old cemeteries at the end of the Canal Street/ Cemeteries streetcar line, the Katrina Mausoleum Memorial is perhaps the least known of the Hurricane Katrina memorials.

Visible from one of the busiest intersections in the city, it sits behind a black metal fence adorned with modern fleur-de-lis motifs, anonymous to the hundreds, if not thousands, of motorists who pass it each day. Most are unaware of its existence.

Seen from above, the memorial is in the shape of a hurricane, with a black granite stele in the middle of an eye formed by the concrete walkway. Two arcs of cypress trees surround the stele, which has a quote of remembrance from the coroner of New Orleans.

To the back of the modestly landscaped property, once a potter's field owned and maintained by Charity Hospital, are six black granite mausoleums containing the remains of scores of unclaimed and unidentified victims of Katrina. After Hurricane Katrina, the remains of unknown citizens were held in warehouses. Organized efforts by the city, the coroner's office, concerned citizens and, most significantly, the New Orleans funerary community, combined to conceive and build the memorial to lay these individuals to rest. Here, as Hurricane Gustav threatened the city in August 2008, a dignified burial was provided to the least recognized victims of the worst man-made disaster in United States history.

The local funerary community, including at least two dozen funeral homes, provided free services that included hearses, pallbearers and all the pomp, circumstance and dignity that distinguishes a New Orleans funeral, complete with a traditional second line for these neglected souls.

To honor the dead, at 9:38am, the time of the first reported levee breach, a bell was tolled three times by dignitaries, including Mayor Ray Nagin and Lt. General Russel Honore. The service ended with an impromptu musical tribute on trumpet from New Orleans coroner Dr. Frank Minyard.

HOLT CEMETERY

A colorful yet poignant celebration of life and death

635 City Park Avenue
Tel: 504-658-3781
Open: 24 hours daily
#91 Jackson/Esplanade bus

n Mid City, behind the right field fence of a baseball diamond, tucked away out of sight to most people, is Holt Cemetery. With no grand mausoleums or expensive monuments, it's not one of New Orleans' renowned above-ground cemeteries. But its tilted headstones, shaded by the boughs of stately moss-draped oaks, provide a colorful yet poignant scene of the city's celebration of life and death. The potter's field is a place for those who have no name or did not have the means to be buried in more traditional resting places.

Opened in 1879 to provide an out of the way spot to allow funeral processions to circumnavigate the city as a precaution against yellow fever and other contagions that made funerals a public hazard, this cemetery was named for Dr. Joseph Holt, an official of the City's Board of Health. He was a pivotal figure in the effort to stem disease in the red-light district known as Storyville.

The modest trappings of a potter's field, which is abundant in artificial flowers, simple tokens of affection and many handmade headstones, does not preclude notable New Orleans personages; among those interred, Holt has its share of the famous, infamous and significant.

The Father of Jazz

The most famous resident of Holt lies in an unmarked grave. Buddy Bolden (1877-1931), who died at the Louisiana Asylum for the Insane in Jackson, Louisiana at age 54, is widely credited by jazz historians as the most influential musician in the early development of jazz. In fact, Bolden is often called the 'Father of Jazz'. Bolden was known throughout New Orleans for his loud, wildly improvisational playing style on his cornet. His band is credited with melding ragtime, blues and church gospel music into what eventually evolved into jazz. Although his grave is unmarked, a commemorative marker was put in the cemetery in 1998.

Another notable laid to rest in Holt is Jessie Hill, the famous rhythm and blues artist best known for the New Orleans classic 'Ooh Poo Pah Doo'. Robert Charles, an African American killed after inciting one of the most notorious race riots in the city's history was originally buried here. Neighbors include Ferris Le Blanc and three unidentified victims of the UpStairs Lounge arson fire in 1973, which is a watershed moment in the struggle for gay rights in the city.

Holt, which is sometimes the site of voodoo rituals, ironically means 'death' in Hungarian.

ALFEREZ ART DECO FENCE ADORNMENTS

An artist who fought in Pancho Villa's army

Tad Gormley Stadium
City Park
5400 Stadium Drive
Tel: 504-482-4888
Open: Tue–Thurs 10am–10pm, Fri–Sat 10am–12am, closed Monday
#91 Jackson/Esplanade bus

I t's possible that almost everyone in New Orleans has passed through the gates of the Tad Gormley Stadium, yet few may have noticed the figures sculpted by artist Enrique Alferez.

His work has been described by art critics as idealistic, democratic and physically and intellectually accessible. These qualities are clearly exhibited in his beloved metal art deco adornments on the gates of Tad Gormley Stadium. The metallic figures are in sets of six repeating forms of men and women in various sporting poses.

The pieces were originally painted black but after a recent renovation and restoration of the stadium, they are now displayed in gleaming gold that catches the light, enhancing the beauty of the works.

Tad Gormley Stadium was built in 1935. The Stadium has since served as the main venue for high school football games in New Orleans. Due to the significance of high school sports in the city's culture, the stadium has a firm place in the personal histories of New Orleans citizens. Many people are personally represented in the stadium by engraved names on the aluminum seats, purchased in order to raise funds to help refurbish the stadium.

Over the years, the stadium has served as a venue for such varied cultural events as the 1992 United States Olympic Trials for Track and Field, an iconic 1964 appearance by The Beatles, religious gatherings, and World War II bond drives hosted by Dorothy Lamour, a native of the city.

Mr. Alferez was the son of Mexican artists and as a young man he actually fought in Pancho Villa's army before coming to the United States to study art in Chicago under Lorado Taft. He moved to New Orleans in 1929 to work for the WPA. Throughout most of the 20th century he continued to leave his mark on both the artistic and physical landscapes of the city.

HISTORIC NEW ORLEANS TRAIN GARDEN ⑦

Fashioned from mosses, twigs, leaves, bark, vines and seeds

5 Victory Avenue
Inside New Orleans Botanical Garden
Tel: 504-483-9488
www.neworleanscitypark.com/botanicalgarden
Open: by admission
Canal streetcar–City Park/Museum or #91 Jackson/Esplanade bus
Trains are limited on Saturdays and Sundays

Tucked away in its own corner of the New Orleans Botanical Garden, under a canopy of tall trees ringed by a serpentine brick walkway laid out to represent water surrounding the city, the City Park Train Garden is a miniature railroad touted as a hidden gem by park literature, slinking around 1,300 feet of model track.

The intricately landscaped route of the model train, built to 1/22 scale, takes it on a journey through a stylized New Orleans of the late 19th or early 20th century, including typical residential architecture, such as camelbacks, shotguns, double shotguns and Creole cottages. The route features familiar landmarks: Lafitte's Blacksmith Shop, St. Louis Cathedral, Lee Circle, and the above ground cemeteries, all rendered in natural plant materials, as is apropos in a botanical garden.

The distinct neighborhoods are represented by buildings you would find while traversing the city. And each stop of the model streetcars has a brief history of that neighborhood.

Paul Busse, a renowned master of what he describes as 'mechanical botanicals', created the railroad garden. Trained as a landscape architect, Busse has designed and built over a hundred similar botanical displays in gardens all over the United States, including Chicago and New York City, where his Christmas Holiday Show attracts thousands each year.

The buildings, which look amazingly true to life, are fashioned from mosses, twigs, leaves, bark, vines and seeds, which are then covered in urethane to protect them from the elements.

Under the magic of Mr. Busse and his artisans, grapevine tendrils become ornamental ironwork, pine cone 'petals' become roof slates, sea grape leaves serve as sidewalk paving, and palm tree husks become porch screens. The effect is startlingly realistic.

The artisans who constructed the buildings included such details as sealing the small plastic windows by pouring a resin casting over them to create a ripple effect, just like old glass of the era.

More recent additions to the dozens of tiny buildings include New Orleans mercantile iconic department stores Maison Blanche and D.H. Holmes in the Canal Street section. These newer additions are not made from botanical materials.

COLOMBIER DE CAROL

A home for pigeons to roost

56 Dreyfous Drive, behind the City Park Casino Building
Tel: 504-482-4888
#91 Jackson/Esplanade bus or Canal streetcar–City Park/Museum

Many Orleanians have probably wondered about the unusual reddish-pink hexagonal brick building that has been sitting behind the City Park casino since 1928. Newly painted since Katrina, it always seems quiet and still. Unless you've ventured across the well-worn bridge that leads to the island it sits upon, you might never guess its purpose. But if you knew the name of the small, rarely visited island, then you might easily guess what it is. Pigeon Island is a pigeonnier - a home for pigeons to roost.

Pigeonniers were designed to provide a haven for the birds. They offer small openings with ledges upon which they could perch safe from predators. The insides of the structures are also built to make it impossible for rats, weasels or foxes to scale to the height where birds might roost.

It is hard to say if pigeons ever made any extensive use of the building and these days the bird-friendly room sits mostly empty except for bird droppings, which were traditionally valued as high-grade fertilizer at the estates where the buildings were housed.

Pigeonniers, also called 'colombiers' or 'dovecotes', were very common at one time across Europe, especially in France, and were also a source of meat and eggs.

Generally, these specially designed structures were the province of the wealthy, who were the only ones allowed to have them. In fact the general population often looked upon them not only as a perk of nobility, but also as a nuisance; often the pigeons were prone to wreak havoc on crops and property of the surrounding countryside. So strong were the feelings on this issue that after the French Revolution, a law was passed to outlaw pigeonniers in France.

The City Park pigeonniers were built by Felix Dreyfous and donated to the park in honor of the birth of his first grandchild, Carol Vera Dreyfous.

THE DUELING OAK

The swashbuckling past of the city

29591 Dreyfous Drive
www.duelingoaks.com
Canal–City Park streetcar or #91 Jackson/Esplanade bus

Next to the New Orleans Museum of Art, only steps from the Sydney and Walda Besthoff Sculpture Garden at City Park, stands a sprawling live oak tree over 300 years old that evokes the romance upon which New Orleans' reputation was built.

Originally, two oaks stood here side by side and came to be called the Dueling Oaks. Below these trees, New Orleans gentlemen came to satisfy affairs of honor. Reasons for duels ranged from rivalry in love to political arguments; fancied slights to mere differences of opinion as to the merits (or lack thereof) of a particular opera. One duel held beneath the oaks was even said to be fought over the trifle of someone's chair being too close to someone else's fiancée at a formal soiree.

Such was the hold of the fashion of dueling (a fashion that could literally kill) that more duels were fought in the city of New Orleans than any other city in America. Just as duels ended with only one man standing, only one of New Orleans' historic Dueling Oaks remains standing today. The other was felled by a hurricane in 1949.

At the time that dueling was the rage, City Park, which rests midway between the Place D'Armes (present-day Jackson Square) and the mouth of Bayou St. John (the main portage of trade goods in the early history of the city), provided a secluded spot far enough away from the populace, thereby giving gentleman a discrete spot to duel.

One of the most prominent citizens of New Orleans, Bernard de Marigny de Mandeville, is said to have fought 19 duels in his lifetime. Another gentleman of New Orleans was recorded as participating in 10 duels in one year. New Orleans' *Times-Democrat* newspaper reported that from 1834 to 1844 scarcely a day passed in the city without a duel.

Dueling was outlawed in 1855, but the 'affairs of honor' continued, although with less frequency, for another 35 years. The last known duel in New Orleans was fought in 1890.

A private cemetery for the victims of a famous duelist

Such were the skills and confidence of famous duelist Señor Don José 'Pepe' Llulla that he is purported to have kept his own private cemetery for his victims. The cemetery is now known as the St. Vincent de Paul Cemetery, also called the Louisa Street Cemetery.

ST. JOHN'S EVE HEAD WASHING CEREMONY

The most important holiday of the Voodoo calendar

Magnolia Bridge on Bayou St. John at Harding Drive
Open: June 23rd, 7pm
Canal–Museum streetcar
#91 Jackson/Esplanade bus, #90 Carrolton bus

Magnolia Bridge, a small footbridge traversing Bayou St. John, is the scene every year of an unusual religious tableau with roots that go back as far as 1719. In the soft summer evening of June 23rd every year, you will find a gathering of Voodoo adherents clad in white, celebrating what many claim is the most important holiday of the Voodoo calendar - St. John's Eve, a feast day dedicated to the most powerful Voodoo spirits and Marie Laveau. The occasion, called *St. John's Eve Head Washing*, is similar to a baptism.

Hundreds of believers gather in the middle of the bridge. The focal point is a large statue of Marie Laveau, the iconic Voodoo priestess of New Orleans, which is surrounded by a tiered altar. By the end of the ceremony, the altar will be almost obscured by offerings. Laveau herself continued this tradition born in the early 18th century on the banks of the bayou that carries the name of St. John the Baptist.

Revelers crowd around the statue of Laveau, led by a machete-wielding disciple who is thought to be opening up the passage from the afterworld on a day considered conducive to crossing the veil.

Sallie Ann Glassman, the modern day Voodoo priestess who revived the tradition in the late 20th century, is also at the center of the ritual. Chanting, drumming and the presentation of offerings swirl around those gathered. Curious bystanders scattered along the bayou look or snap photos, while others in kayaks or canoes paddle up to partake in the spectacle. Indeed, it is a welcoming celebration, open to the public, who may walk right up and into the crowd of revelers as long as they are respectful.

Offerings to the spirit world are an integral part of the practice of Voodoo. They are given up to Lwa, a powerful spirit of the afterworld, to ensure a propitious worldly year to the supplicant. On this day, items offered have a decided flavor to please Ms. Laveau's taste: Creole dishes, flowers, gris gris bags, blue and white candles, Florida water and hair dressing supplies - the latter because Laveau was a hairdresser.

As evening becomes night, Ms. Glassman prepares the liquid for the head washing. It is a concoction of flowers, fruits such as strawberries and dates, and even a whole coconut cake, all mashed together and applied to devotees' heads, which are then wrapped in a white scarf not to be removed until morning. The ceremony ends with a procession led by Glassman that snakes back and forth across Magnolia Bridge as the crowd chants *"Aiyobo"* - the Vodun equivalent of 'amen'.

THE OLDEST FIRE HYDRANT IN NEW ORLEANS

Water pumped directly from the bayou to fight fires

Corner of Moss Street and Grande Route St. John
#91 Jackson/Esplanade bus or City Park streetcar

At the corner of Moss Street and Grand Route St. John, just steps from Bayou St. John, what could be mistaken for a bit of modern industrial design but for its well-oxidized patina, is in fact a fire hydrant; one that marked an important breakthrough in firefighting history.,

Manufactured in 1869 in Lockport New York, this Birdsill Holly hydrant is the oldest fire hydrant in New Orleans. Long since retired, it has somehow survived to give a glimpse into early urban fire fighting techniques.

Since the city of New Orleans did not have a public water system until late into the 19th century, it can be surmised that the proximity to the bayou of the old hydrant made it possible for a fire company to draft water from Bayou St. John through the hydrant. The fire pump could then supply the necessary water pressure to extinguish the fire.

The advantage to the fire fighters was that they could position their apparatus closer to the scene, thus enabling a more rapid attack on the fire.

Birdsill Holly, whose count of U.S. patents was second only to Thomas Edison's, specialized in fire protection systems early in his career. Some even gave him credit for the invention of the fire hydrant. However, other hydrants predate Holly's patents.

Holly's fire protection systems and water delivery designs were eventually used in over 2,000 American and Canadian cities. His impact on fire prevention was considerable.

Early on, the president of the Holly Company was so confident in his product that the firm made a promise of an indemnity to anyone whose taxes were not offset by the reduced fire insurance on their properties.

The date of the patent (1869, marked clearly on the hydrant) is also of some interest, in that Holly's hydrant system wasn't adopted by Chicago until years later in the aftermath of the Great Chicago Fire of 1871.

MUSIC TREE

A totem to the renewal of New Orleans

On the bank of Bayou St. John near the intersection of Moss Street and Orleans Avenue
Canal streetcar or #91 Jackson/Esplanade bus

At the south end of Bayou St. John, near to its intersection with Orleans Avenue, a dead oak tree has become a work of art. It is the work of master chainsaw artist Marlin Miller, who has created similar works all over the United States. The tree sports a keyboard on its trunk, a fiddle and a guitar on one side, and a pelican on another.

Miller chose to preserve the narrow branches at the top of the tree by carving birds in flight.

After the initial shaping of the tree, he burnishes the surface with a torch to add depth and then varnishes it; the varnish seeps into the tree to preserve both the image and the wood itself. Finally, it is treated to protect it from termites.

Miller receives numerous requests to apply his magic to trees, so he must pick and choose his subjects carefully. He has specific criteria that a tree must meet to qualify for his beautiful makeovers: it must be hardwood; it must be on public property; it must be in a highly visible area; and it must have some emotion tied to it. Miller said that the tree at the end of Bayou St. John met all of these requirements "perfectly".

This tree, called the 'Music Tree', actually survived the wind and flooding of Katrina only to succumb to a lightning strike during Hurricane Isaac in 2012.

The artful transformation of the tree was at the behest of organizers of the Mid-City Bayou Boogaloo, a free neighborhood music and arts festival, wishing to focus attention on the replanting of trees along the bayou. Proceeds from the festival have gone toward repopulating the bayou with trees lost to time and hurricanes.

> The tree stands as a solitary sentinel all year round, except for one weekend when the shores of the bayou become a fairground for a free music festival.

3127 PONCE DE LEON STREET ART GALLERY ⑬

A curious art gallery that has no name

3127 Ponce de Leon Street
#90 Jackson/Esplanade bus

I f you walk down the sidewalk past the residences of Ponce de Leon Street toward Esplanade, at number 3127, through a glass door with no signage, you'll see a bare art installation. This downstairs space of a two-storey building is a curious gallery that has no name.

The gallery is the handiwork of Joe Cabral, a well-known New Orleans musician and member of the popular band The Iguanas.

Cabral has taken advantage of the space in a creative, whimsical way. The property is owned by a friend who allows Cabral to use it to its best advantage - which he initially did by selling furniture through Craigslist. It then occurred to him that the space could be utilized for an art installation, as the medium had always intrigued him.

His mind started churning toward this goal and the discovery of several yellow cubes he came across at Habitat for Humanity became the impetus for his first exhibit.

He then decided to play with 28 yellow volumes by setting them up in a certain configuration - an iteration, as he calls it.

As time passed he would rearrange the volumes. People started to take notice, with an air of curiosity at first; it seemed as if an unseen hand was changing the pattern of whatever it was, lending a subversive element to the experiment. Cabral was happy with the results and started to ponder his next step.

This led to a new iteration of plywood shipping crates he got from a local artist. The mysterious installation art had by this time caught the neighborhood's imagination.

An eye-level metal construct that cut the room in half (and also cut off access to the room) was next.

Cabral has since hosted shows of another artist whose work he felt was simpatico with his, before going back to his own installations, using bamboo from his yard to create the next artistic statement.

The statement is open ended, continuously evolving and slowly seeping into the ethos of this bustling urban neighborhood. Cabral says with great pride and enthusiasm that the works here are open to any interpretation.

"They mean what you want them to mean."

LULING MANSION

The most beautiful house in the South

1436 Leda Court
Private residence not open to the public
#91 Jackson/Esplanade bus or Canal–Museum streetcar

At the end of Esplanade Avenue as you approach City Park traveling from the river, the old boulevard sparkles with beautiful mansions, many over a century old. But the star, and once the finest home in New Orleans, lurks just off the avenue obscured from view, even to those who know it's there.

Now a run-down apartment building, the mansion was designed by James Gallier Jr., one of New Orleans most esteemed architects, and built in 1865 by cotton merchant Florence Luling, all for the princely sum of $24,000 - the equivalent of at least a few million dollars today.

Although it has obviously seen better days, it still boasts a regal bearing with balconies, galleries, arched windows and a large stairway leading to the front door overlooking a lawn that once fronted on Esplanade Avenue. It still has the power to inspire awe when seen by unsuspecting eyes. Modeled after an Italian Renaissance Palace, the property once encompassed 80 acres, which included it sown lake. Shortly after moving in, the Lulings were struck with tragedy when their two sons drowned in Bayou St. John only a few blocks away. They left New Orleans never to return and sold the property to the Louisiana Jockey Club, which had just purchased the adjacent Creole Racetrack. The club opened the Fair Grounds Racetrack the next year in 1872.

The Jockey Club became a legendary party destination, with lavish banquets, carnival masquerades and what were described as extravagant cocktail parties. These social affairs were attended by a who's who of New Orleans society as well as important dignitaries visiting the city.

The notables included Ulysses S. Grant, Edgar Degas and Grand Duke Alexis of Russia. The Jockey Club sold the property in 1905, citing the expense of the upkeep. It was converted into eight apartments, some of which are still in use. Today, the old grand dame of a building stands a bit pared back. Some of its outbuildings are gone and much of the luxurious grounds of yesteryear have been sold. The once extensive parcel of land was subdivided into residential lots, some of which now serve to shield its view from the passing traffic. But the mansion itself remains, in all its crumbling glory, as a proud reminder of a different age.

RESIDENCE ON ESPLANADE AVE., NEW ORLEANS, LA.

SINGING OAK

Largest wind chime sculpture in America

On Big Lake in City Park near the intersection of Lelong Avenue and Wisner Blvd.
www.neworleanscitypark.com
Canal streetcar–City Park/Museum
#91 Jackson/Esplanade bus
#90 Carrolton bus

The Singing Oak consists of seven wind chimes tuned to play as one hidden inside a 180-year-old oak tree. The largest chime is 14 feet long and the smallest is 30 inches.

As wind blows through the canopy the chimes catch lake breezes coming down Bayou St. John, which serves as one of the park's boundaries. The chimes are painted black to blend in with the natural shadow of the oaks and are tuned to the major pentatonic scale, the predominant scale used in West African music. It was this music that inspired spirituals, gospel, jazz, blues and even rock 'n' roll.

The flood caused by the failure of the federally maintained levees during Hurricane Katrina inundated the park, damaging or killing many of the trees. Artist Jim Hart created the chimes and placed them in one of the remaining trees in the John S. McIlhilleny Meadow. The meadow is located near the east end of Big Lake.

The seventh most visited urban park in the United States, City Park inhabits a natural fulcrum of New Orleans historic real estate. It is home to the oldest grove of mature live oaks in the world; some of them are said to be 900 years old. Curiously enough, one of the newest attractions at the park is also located in one of these ancient trees.

Indigenous to the southern United States, the live oak ranges from Virginia to Florida in the east and along the gulf coast to Mexico; it is one of the more striking, accessible and ubiquitous natural wonders of New Orleans. Thanks to the foresight of generations of city planners, the city's boulevards are graced by hundreds of stately examples.

Today, this ancient tree serves as a peaceful melodic respite; a place for people to meet, lunch, visit or just contemplate the day.

WAVE OF THE WORLD FOUNTAIN

A work of art lost for 30 years finally returns

On Big Lake in City Park near the intersection of LeLong Avenue and Wisner Blvd.
www.neworleanscitypark.com
Canal streetcar–City Park/Museum
#90 Jackson/Esplanade bus, #91 Carrolton bus

At the bank of Big Lake in City Park surrounded by a small forest of reeds, 'The Wave of the World' is a fountain sculpted by internationally known artist Lynda Benglis. The intriguing story of this beautiful work is reminiscent of the satirical novel *A Confederacy of Dunces*, the celebrated work of fiction set in New Orleans.

The fountain has traveled across the Atlantic and back and has been exhibited in front of a casino in Monaco just after the fair. Yet it has spent much of the past several decades languishing.

Winner of a competition to create art for the 1984 New Orleans World's Fair under the theme 'Fresh Water as a Source of Life', Ms. Benglis' fountain was purchased by businessman Carl Eberts for $100,000 at the behest of his daughters (with a grant of $15,000 that required it to be displayed to the public). After the first blush of ownership, Mr. Eberts was at a loss as to where to display the piece, so he donated it to the city of Kenner. At that point, it disappeared from the consciousness of the city. It was left in a kind of bureaucratic purgatory and became lost for over thirty years. All the while it stood in plain sight in a yard next to the city's sewage treatment plant.

"Nobody knew what it was," said Mike Quigley, Kenner's Chief Administrative Officer. Which begs the question, 'how did it get into the unknowing hands of the City of Kenner?'. The answer turned out to be that the former mayor of Kenner and later the Parish President of Jefferson Parish, who later ended up in prison for some kind of malfeasance, happened to be Mr Eberts brother-in-law and it was he who in a burst of civic mindedness proposed that it be donated to the city. "We didn't know what it was worth," said Kenner mayor Mike Yenni. About a million dollars as it turns out.

Ms. Benglis had inquired about the whereabouts of a work she held dear to her heart. Finally, thanks to her persistance, diligent attorneys, a local art dealer, and the curator of the New Orleans Museum Of Art, the fountain found its way back into the public's consciousness after a detour via Ms. Benglis' studios to be repaired. Now on loan to the park, with the assistance of the New Orleans-based Helis Foundation, the sculpture is again delighting visitors.

POPP'S FOUNTAIN

A spectacular 30-foot spray in the air

12 Magnolia Drive
Tel: 504-482-4888
www.neworleanscitypark.com
Open: 10am–10pm
#45 Lakeview bus (closest public transit)

At this rarely visited landmark in the less-traveled northern side of City Park, the sound of Popp's Fountain's multiple water plumes competes with the constant whirr of automobiles on the busy interstate highway only steps away.

A 60-foot circular fountain built in 1937 by the WPA, Popp's Fountain is surrounded by 26 Corinthian columns connected at the top by a wooden trellis adorned with flowing foliage. It has seen its ups and downs since its inception, but today it has new life; the 12-acre park in which it stands has been fully renovated and landscaped with plants, shrubs and native trees, creating a lush contemplative space. The newly constructed Arbor Room makes it a perfect site for events such as weddings.

Featuring leaping dolphins around a metal lotus centerpiece designed by Enrique Alferez, the art deco fountain shoots a spectacular 30-foot spray into the air.

For all its beauty and efforts to refurbish and update it, the spot remains a quiet refuge in the park on most days. Visitors will often find themselves alone, or one of very few, on any given day.

The fountain was first funded by Rebecca Grant Popp and her sister, with a donation of $25,000 in 1929, to honor Mrs. Popp's husband, who died an untimely death. The fountain is named in Mr. Popp's memory. The original plan for the monument was created by the Olmstead Brothers in 1929.

Witchcraft in the fountain

In the 1970s, the fountain was so neglected that it became a spot used by a local witch to hold rituals. Popp's Fountain in those days was derelict, unfenced and open. Local witch Mary Oneida practiced meditation in the area and eventually used the 60-foot circular fountain with its tiered walkways for witchcraft ceremonies. The coven led by Ms. Oneida, The Religious Order of Witchcraft, was the first to be recognized as a 'church' by the state of Louisiana. Ms. Oneida died in 1981, but some say that strange things still occur at the fountain.

LABORDE MOUNTAIN

The new highest elevation in New Orleans

Just off Harrison Avenue near intersection with Marconi Avenue
Inside Couturie Forest
www.neworleanscitypark.com
Open: daylight hours
Nearest bus #45 Lakeview or #91 Jackson/Esplanade

Laborde Mountain in City Park, the new highest elevation in New Orleans, stands just inside Couturie Forest, across the reddish bridge near the new entrance on the Harrison Avenue parking lot.

Entering the forest from the gravel lot, follow one of the dirt paths until you come to a fork in the path then bear left. As you continue deeper into the forest, you see the ground rise up ahead. A crushed brick and soil ascent leads you up to the summit, which is referred to as 'Laborde Lookout'. At the lookout (which once sported a deck constructed of cypress logs laid in a mosaic design) you will find a metal grate-like floor surrounded by a half circle of graffiti marked benches that seem to have been burned or vandalized in some way; it's not a very picturesque sight.

From the vantage point of the mountain, the canopy of the high trees obscures the rest of the forest. Two other descents, one a concrete shard path and the other made of tiered railroad ties, bring you to the other paths that wind through the forest and its eight eco-systems.

New Orleans is a notoriously flat landscape with significant areas in the city below sea level, as was dramatically demonstrated by the flood waters of Hurricane Katrina, which inundated the park. Monkey Hill, an Audubon Park landmark that rises to a 15 foot elevation on the opposite side of the city, was built by the Civil Works Administration in the 1930s. It had been the highest point in the city for several generations.

Couturie Forest is a 60-acre nature preserve incorporating trails, scenic waterways and a wildlife refuge. It is also said to be one of the best places to watch birds inside the city limits. The park was devastated by Katrina and most of Couterie Forest, built by the CWA in 1938, is the result of extensive planning and planting after Katrina.

If you want to be alone in a natural environment within the city, Couterie Forest is your ticket.

A man-made hill

Laborde Mountain is a man-made hill constructed of rip-rap left over from construction of interstate 610 in the 1960s, a project that was not finished until the 1970s due to environmental lawsuits. The 'mountain' was named after Ellis Laborde who was the long time general manager of City Park.

ASHTRAY HOUSE

A house made of 1,200 glass ashtrays

28 Park Island Drive
Private residence not open to the public
#51 St. Bernard–St. Anthony bus

I f houses could talk, the unusually adorned modernist residence at 28 Park Island Drive would have tales many would enjoy hearing. On a quiet turn in the street on Park Island, it is an exclusive residential piece of New Orleans, surrounded by a winding Bayou St. John, accessible only via a small bridge, where 99.9% of local citizens will likely never set foot.

It is the exterior embellishments that make this house such a curiosity. The entire perimeter is clad near the roofline with around 1,200 identical amber glass ashtrays embedded into the stucco walls.

In an interview about the unusual use of ashtrays in the design, Mr Ledner said that the couple who commissioned him loved to smoke, hence the use of ashtrays as an architectural motif.

The house is the work of renowned New Orleans modernist architect Albert Ledner, who, after graduating from Tulane University, apprenticed at Taliesin under Frank Lloyd Wright.

Ledner is known for innovative and creative designs and many homes in New Orleans bear his distinctive, offbeat touches. Among them is a house with light fixtures fashioned from Cointreau liquor bottles; another has light fixtures made from pop-top Schlitz beer cans. He also has structures of note outside New Orleans, such as three nautical-themed buildings he designed for the National Maritime Union in New York City, one of which was renovated into the Maritime Hotel in 2003.

There is one more interesting piece of New Orleans culture connected to Mr. Ledner - his mother Beulah's role in the introduction of a well-loved local treat. During the depression, Beulah's family owned the bakery where a New Orleans version of the Austro-Hungarian Dobos torte dessert was created, thereby inventing the Doberge cake, known to all Orleanians as a staple of our culinary heritage.

The Park Island home's more recent claim to fame is that it was the residence of C. Ray Nagin, the mayor of New Orleans at the time of Hurricane Katrina. Nagin became a national and international figure in the aftermath of the storm and the catastrophic flood it unleashed on New Orleans. Nagin was a lightning rod in New Orleans for his public remarks about race and for his leadership (or lack thereof) in his second term as mayor. He has the distinction of being the first mayor in almost 300 years of New Orleans history to be indicted and convicted of bribery. Nagin's indictment and the expense of his trial led the former mayor to sell the Park Island residence in 2012.

HIGGINS THERMO-CON HOME

Thermo-Con, touted as a modern wonder material

30 Tern Street
Open: Private residence, not open to the public
#45 Lakeview bus

L iterally only a couple of hundred yards from Lake Pontchartrain, a white International Style mansion sitting off the beaten path in an exclusive nook of Lake Vista is one of the few tangible reminders of a failed experiment by one of New Orleans' more storied entrepreneurs.

Built by Andrew Higgins as his personal residence, the house was designed to showcase his invention, Thermo-Con, a modern building material he hoped would revolutionize construction post-World War II.

Recent owners of the home have done much upkeep, scrupulously adhering to Higgins' vision.

They have been greatly assisted by the fact that the home came with a complete set of original plans. Original materials have been used whenever possible and finer details, such as the mahogany doors and double helix interior staircase, have been preserved. Also still present is a wet bar that Higgins installed, fashioned out of the stern of an LCVP landing craft that hit the beach at Normandy.

From all accounts by occupants of the home over the years, Thermo-Con has delivered on its promise of strength, durability, and insulation. Thermo-Con, touted as a modern wonder material, was a combination of Portland cement, water, aluminum flakes, caustic soda and bituminous emulsion.

The mixture was poured into a mold and would rise in a process similar to baking. This process produced a gas-expanded cellular composition with a very high strength-to-weight ratio.

Thermo-Con was fire-resistant, moisture-proof and vermin-proof, with low heat and cold transmission and high heat insulation properties. Another advantage was that it boasted wood-like characteristics, making it extremely versatile. All these positive selling points enticed the U.S. Army to sign a contract with Higgins' corporation to build prototypes, in order to develop a standard house design to meet the army's housing shortage. But the idea never caught on and very few structures built with Thermo-Con remain. One that has survived is at Fort Belvoir in Virginia; it still houses visiting dignitaries and was designated a historic landmark by the state of Virginia.

Andrew Higgins was also the founder of Higgins Industries, the New Orleans-based manufacturer of the Higgins boat (LCVP) during World War II. General Dwight D. Eisenhower once proclaimed him as the man who won World War II because of the importance of his landing boats, built in New Orleans and delivered to soldiers in battle, including the Normandy landing on D-Day.

SPANISH FORT

The Coney Island of the South

Beauregard Avenue just steps away from intersection of Robert E. Lee Blvd. and Wisner Blvd.
#47 Cemeteries bus

Spanish Fort, the almost nondescript ruin near the intersection of Robert E. Lee and Wisner Boulevards is a perfect spot for a picnic. But the current scene lying across the street from a quiet prosperous neighborhood belies a much more colorful history.

Today, only a few bricks, a plaque and a solitary grave are all that is left as testament to the important role this piece of real estate once played in both the leisure and commerce of early New Orleans.

The original French fort was constructed on the spot where Bienville and Iberville set up camp in 1699, 19 years before the founding of New Orleans.

The fort, or what's left of it, occupies a strategic location at what was the mouth of Bayou St. John.

Before the mouth of the bayou was closed during a 20th-century land reclamation project, Bayou St. John was an essential artery for trade throughout most of the city's history. The city was much more accessible to ocean going vessels via Lake Pontchartrain. The portages from the bayou near what is now Esplanade Avenue served as one of the main avenues of trade into the city.

The Spanish rebuilt the original fortifications in 1779, hence the name. And the fort was refurbished again by the Americans in 1808.

Shortly after the American renovations, the area became popular with New Orleans residents due to the cooling lake breezes. It became a popular recreation spot that included a luxury hotel, several fine restaurants, a dance hall, a casino, and an amusement park. The area flourished from 1823 until the early 20th century.

Luminaries such as Oscar Wilde, Ulysses S. Grant and William Makepeace Thackery either appeared or were guests at the resort. So popular was the complex it was dubbed 'The Coney Island of the South'.

The Confederate forces manned the fort in the early stages of the Civil War to protect the city from a Union invasion. During the short-lived garrison of Confederate troops, inventor Horace Lawson Hunley built the world's first 'torpedo boat', or submarine, at the Spanish Fort. The vessel sank, killing three soldiers. But later in the war, Hunley built another submarine; in Charleston Bay in 1864, the CSS Hunley became the first submarine to sink an enemy ship.

LOUP GAROU STATUE

(22)

Unapologetic in all regards... honest, coarse, ugly and powerful

2000 Lakeshore Drive
Tel: 504-280-6000
www.uno.edu
#52 St. Bernard-Paris bus or #55 Elysian Fields bus

At nearly 104 tons and 33 feet high, a massive concrete sculpture seems unlikely to be considered a secret. Nonetheless, Peter Lundberg's thrice-named work "Loup Garou," standing for all to see on the University of New Orleans (UNO) campus across the street from the Fine Arts Gallery, fits the bill.

UNO is situated on Lake Pontchartrain and is thereby not one of the more visited parts of the city. The placement of the huge work of art finds it in one of the least traversed parts of the campus, on a dead end street to boot, that sees little to no automobile traffic on any given day.

Vermont-based sculptor Lundberg created his piece in New Orleans by digging a hole in the backyard of a former molasses plant in Bywater then filling the void first with rebar, tires, industrial cables and miscellaneous debris before adding lots of concrete. An industrial crane raised the massive result, which was then entitled "Mississippi Gateway."

The sculpture was moved to City Park near the New Orleans Museum of Art, but the soft ground at the park proved an unwelcoming host, not allowing for a stable base. For a time, the work laid on its side until it was moved to another destination on UNO's campus. Again its base seemed unstable and it was eventually moved across Harwood Drive to a new custom-made base, where it stands today.

After its latest move, the cost alone of moving the work was approximately $145,000, almost equal to its estimated worth of $150,000. The work was described by one art professor as "unapologetic in all regards... honest, coarse, ugly and powerful."

Lundberg renamed the piece "Mississippi Passage" some time later. His custom in the past has been to name his work after mythological creatures, so after becoming familiar with the French Louisiana werewolf myth of Loup Garou he settled on the present name.

KING LEAR STATUE

King Lear in an anxious hollow eyed pose

2000 Lakeshore Drive
Tel: 504-280-6000
www.uno.edu
#55 Elysian Fields bus

The 20 foot high statue of King Lear made out of fiberglass, plastic foam and steel that stands in front of the Performing Arts Building at the University of New Orleans (UNO) is one of the least known works of art in the city. Surprisingly, only a handful of Orleanians could tell you where it is or what it is.

UNO is a community college situated next to Lake Pontchartrain with a small number of students living on campus. Only those who have business on campus come into contact with the statue. At first glance, its size and the visual effect of the swirls and folds of the design make it difficult to tell exactly what it is.

The pewter-toned work depicts what appears to be a youthful Lear in an anxious, hollow-eyed pose looking down at his fingers, seemingly searching his own thoughts.

The statue was formerly displayed in Washington, DC, and in Chicago. It is the work of New Jersey-based sculptor Seward Johnson, grandson of Robert Johnson, the founder of medical and pharmaceutical company *Johnson & Johnson*. On loan to the university, the statue was shipped to New Orleans in two pieces via flatbed truck in September of 2011.

Seward Johnson is best known for his trompe l'oeil painted bronze statues that are fabricated by technicians from castings of live people. Another of his noted works is "The Awakening" (1980). It is his largest and most dramatic piece, depicting a giant trying to free himself from under the ground.

Johnson's 1982 work "Double Check" received a lot of publicity. The statue depicting a businessman checking his briefcase was located across from the World Trade Center in New York City on 11 September 2001. Images of it covered in debris after the terrorist attacks were beamed across the world on television that day. It later received more public attention after being relocated to Zuccotti Park in 2006, where it again made news as it was adorned by Occupy Wall Street protestors.

OUR LADY OF LAVANG MISSION

A postcard in memory of a miracle
in the Vietnamese jungle

6054 Vermillion Blvd.
Tel: 504-283-0559
www.lavangshrine.net
#55 Elysian Fields bus or #51 St. Bernard-St. Anthony bus

Located at the site of a former Lutheran church in a working class neighborhood that was ravaged by hurricane Katrina, Our Lady of La Vang Mission is a Vietnamese shrine standing several storeys tall, topped by a statue of Our Lady of LaVang. A raised altar sits above two circular tiered pools of water and occasionally serves in outdoor services of the church that occupies this space. Every Mother's Day, the grounds are also home to the Festival of Our Lady of LaVang.

The site looks as if it belongs on a Vietnamese postcard. Indeed, with mass schedules and most signage clearly in Vietnamese, this church is among several in New Orleans that serve the large Vietnamese community: after the fall of Vietnam in 1976, many Vietnamese fled the communist regime and settled in the United States. There are now approximately two dozen Catholic churches that bear the name of Our Lady of LaVang today in the United States. Due to the similarity of the New Orleans climate to their homeland and the proximity of the fishing industry, many Vietnamese found new homes in New Orleans. Another key reason for the settlement in New Orleans was New Orleans Archbishop Philip Hannan, the first Catholic archbishop to visit Fort Chafee in Arkansas where the first refugees were sent. Through the work of Catholic charities, Archbishop Hannan resettled over 1,000 families on that first trip. In 1974 there were almost zero Vietnamese in the city. Today there are over 15,000. The New Orleans Vietnamese community has flourished in the city and boasts Joseph Cao, the first United States congressman of Vietnamese heritage, as one of their own.

A Vietnamese tree and the apparition of Virgin Mary

The shrine gets its name from an incident deep in the Vietnamese rainforest at the end of the 18th century. The emperor of Annam had issued an anti-Catholic edict and the faithful fled into the forest and congregated at one particular tree every night to pray the rosary. One night up in a branch of that tree, an apparition of a lady dressed in traditional Vietnamese garb and holding an infant in her arms instructed those assembled to boil the leaves of the tree as a medicine to combat illnesses that had befallen them. As word spread, that place became a holy site for Vietnamese Catholics and a chapel was built here to honor Our Lady. Persecutions continued over the years with an estimated 100,000 Catholics being martyred between 1700 and 1800. In Vietnam, the Basilica of Our Lady of La Vang is situated in what is today Hai Phu commune in Hai Lăng District of Quang Tri Province in Central Vietnam. *La* means 'leaf' and *Vang* means 'grass seed'.

LAKEFRONT AIRPORT TERMINAL MURALS ㉕

A riot of art deco design

6001 Stars and Stripes Blvd.
Tel: 504-243-4010
www.lakefrontairport.com
Terminal open daily 7am–4:30pm
#60 Hayne bus

The striking pastel yellow bas-relief exterior of the New Orleans Lakefront Airport gives only a hint of the opulent interior that awaits the visitor to this time capsule of a building.

The architectural detail seems endless: a marble staircase; chandeliers out of a Dashiell Hammet novel; the geometric-patterned inlaid ceiling; a vintage neon sign pointing toward the dining room; and stylized metalwork skirting the balcony. Even the coffee shop stools drip with the crisp lines of the era.

A compass in the center of a terrazzo floor points to every corner of the globe and specifically to the Xavier Gonzalez murals that adorn the walls of the balcony, celebrating the history of human flight.

Of the eight murals that were originally created, only seven survive; the eighth canvas, entitled *Flight over Bali*, has been severely damaged. The murals, depicting famous flights in aviation history, including Admiral Richard Byrd's flight over the South Pole and Lindbergh's groundbreaking flight to Paris, were restored in 2015-16 by experts brought in from all over the country.

One thing you can safely say about Gov. Huey Long, who ruled Louisiana like an emperor in the 1920s and 30s, is that he never thought small, especially when it came to public works. The Louisiana Capitol building, the massive art deco Charity Hospital and the Mississippi River Bridge, now named after him, all attest to that. But his ambitions were never more artistically expressed than in the airport that he commissioned and opened in 1934 as a state-of-the-art airline terminal. Today, the newly restored building at Lakefront Airport is testament to Long's vision; a riot of artistic design, it is thought to be the first modern art deco land and sea airport.

Huey Long and his appointed Levee Board president Abe Shushan built the airport on a sliver of reclaimed land jutting out into Lake Pontchartrain. This made for wide views for pilots. It also conveniently placed the glittering terminal and runways just outside New Orleans' jurisdiction. Having feuded with the city's politicians for years, Long's maneuver gave him and his proxy, Shushan, full control. The airport was originally named after Shushan, who had carte blanche to achieve their vision without interference.

The airport served New Orleans as its primary airport from 1934 to 1946, until city fathers had their revenge by building Moisant Airport, 20 miles away in a neighboring parish. However, Lakefront Airport remains one of the busiest general aviation airports in the United States.

ABANDONED SIX FLAGS AMUSEMENT PARK

Disney World in Hell

3011 Michoud Blvd.
Tel: 504-253-8108 ext 3333
Closed to the public
No near public transportation

Rising out of the vast wetlands in New Orleans East, the spine of an abandoned roller coaster juts from the horizon just to your right as you head east on Interstate 10.

This is the site of Six Flags New Orleans, the former modern amusement park destroyed by Hurricane Katrina. The grounds of the park and its attractions sat swamped by brackish water for more than a month after the storm.

The abandoned Mega Zeph, The Big Easy, and Muskrat Rambler rides still tower over the midway, litter-strewn and covered with fading graffiti. The attractions now sit behind padlocked gates and are off limits to sightseers, mainly due to the danger presented by the condition of the place and the threat of wild animals. Yet the size and height of the structures allows the decay to be seen clearly from a distance.

Although trespassing is strictly forbidden, some intrepid urban explorers continue to invade the property in search of thrills and to take pictures of the ghostly landscape of the rusty, deteriorating campus. What they find is a nightmarish ruin, a Disney World in Hell.

The eerie setting is only a few thousand yards from the highway; skeletal remains of gnarled and twisted steel, weathered rides and decaying wood thrust into the sky, providing the perfect backdrop for to an apocalyptic horror movie.

Several attempts to revive the attraction have been floated, including several to refurbish and expand it as an amusement park and even one to turn it into an outlet mall. But none have come to fruition and the property, now owned by the City of New Orleans, seems destined to remain the go-to spot for major movie projects in Louisiana's growing film industry. Movies including *Dawn of the Planet of the Apes*, *Jurassic World* and *Percy Jackson: Sea of Monsters* have been filmed there.

New Orleans East is a huge expanse of land that was opened up to large development in the 1960s with great fanfare and promise. Yet even before Katrina, the area's better days were behind it. Judging by the abandoned park now sitting at the eastern edge of this area, it seems as if all dreams of development are being swallowed up by sinking soil and encroaching wetlands.

ISLEÑOS MUSEUM

*The memory of immigrants who came
from the Canary Islands*

1345 Bayou Road, St. Bernard, Louisiana
Tel: 504-277-4681
www.losislenos.org
Open: Wed–Sun 11am–4pm and by appointment

I n a picture perfect rural setting on Bayou Road in St. Bernard, among wooden houses and stately moss-covered oaks, the Los Isleños Heritage and Multi-Cultural Park is a museum that is really a small complex of historic buildings. Most of the buildings were once inhabited by residents of St. Bernard Parish, who can trace their ancestors directly to the first immigrants to arriving in Louisiana from the Canary Islands in 1778.

The first building of the complex was designed by architects in the spirit of the homes built by the ancestors of the first Isleños. It is equipped with artifacts such as traditional clothes, utensils, tools and other items of everyday use. Many of the items were donated by the Spanish government after the devastation of the complex by Hurricane Katrina.

Next to this building is the DuCros House which serves as a library and meeting room. The house showcases the outdoor culture established here with an emphasis on trapping, hunting and fishing. There are dugout pirogues - the small boats Native Americans showed the first Isleños how to construct to help navigate the swampy bayous.

Other smaller houses that were moved to the park demonstrate the historic architecture of the Isleños.

Two identical houses are built in the typical floor plan and are constructed in a traditional manner. One is up-to-date, the other is left as it may have been when inhabited years ago, with cypress posts and bousillage construction. Bousillage (made from mud, moss and hair) was used as insulation in early southern Louisiana.

Moved here and reassembled just as it was when it was a hub of social and commercial gatherings in the community, the Coconut Barroom is a small rustic bar that can be rented for private events.

A replica of a trapping cabin built by a former trapper, complete with hanging muskrat pelts, gives a real flavor of how it must have been to work this land. There is also a palmetto hut donated by the Houmas Tribe, showing how Native Americans lived in these environs.

Every year the complex is the site of the Los Isleños Festival.

SEVEN SISTERS OAK

*Limbs twisting high and wide in a pose akin
to interpretive dance*

200 Fountain Street, Lewisburg, Louisiana
www.lgcfinc.org/live-oak-society.html

In Lewisburg, a suburb of Mandeville near the shore of Lake Pontchartrain, the limbs of a magnificent live oak tree reach upward and outward, twisting high and wide, as if seeking something. In a pose akin to interpretive dance, it stands in the place it has occupied for perhaps a thousand years or more.

At 67 feet high and 130 feet in diameter, with a girth last measured at nearly 40 feet, the Seven Sisters Oak is the largest live oak in the south. Estimated to be between 500 and 1500 years old, it holds the title of National Champion Live Oak and has been designated the President of the Live Oak Society (whose members are all trees), an honor it has held since 1968.

Located on private property, the oak was a matter of disputed authenticity for a time as many claimed it was actually not one but perhaps several oaks that had grown together over the years to appear as one tree.

However, in 1976 all doubt was dispelled when a team of federal foresters inspected the tree and found a single root system.

The name Seven Sisters has several origin stories. One says the tree is named for its seven limbs, although there are actually more than seven branches extending out and up. Another claims that the owners of the property on which the oak stands had seven daughters, hence the Seven Sisters appellation. Yet another claims it is derived from a Choctaw name lost to history.

Lewisburg sits on the banks of Lake Pontchartrain, to the left after you cross the Causeway from New Orleans. It is a tiny, lesser-known and lesser-traveled part of Mandeville. Although it has been there for many years, it remains something of a secret, as even many Orleanians who are asked to locate it are at a loss. This also adds to the relative obscurity of this huge and important tree.

Originally Choctaw land, Lewisburg is a historic property. Catholic Father Adrien-Emmanuel Rouquette, the first native of Louisiana to be ordained a priest, sermonized and converted many of the Native Americans with whom he had enjoyed a close relationship since his childhood. He was known to have attempted to translate the Bible into Choctaw and indeed was bestowed the Choctaw name *Chata-Ima* (Choctaw-like). In this area, perhaps under the canopy of this very tree, he is believed to have ministered to his newly converted flock.

DEW DROP SOCIAL & BENEVOLENT ㉙ JAZZ HALL

The oldest intact jazz hall in the world

438 Lamarque Street
Mandeville, Louisiana
Email: dewdropjazzhall@hotmail.com
www.dewdropjazzhall.com

The Dew Drop Social & Benevolent Jazz Hall is an old, weathered, unpainted wooden building surrounded by moss-covered oaks on Lamarque Street in the old part of Mandeville. It looks every bit the abandoned rural southern church, but it is arguably one of the most historically significant music venues in America.

Most of the year it is locked down. Sitting idle, it appears like a southern gothic canvas out of central casting. But for a dozen or so times a year, it comes alive to fulfil its original purpose as a place to perform concerts and listen to the joyful noise of jazz.

The Dew Drop Benevolent Society was created in 1885 by civic-minded African Americans to fill a need in the their community for services not available through insurance. The society's goals were to care for the sick, to provide food and housing and to offer financial assistance for members in need.

In 1895, a cornerstone was laid. The present day building opened the same year, making the Dew Drop Social and Benevolent Jazz Hall the oldest intact jazz hall in the world.

Almost immediately after its opening, jazz musicians from New Orleans started to sail across Lake Pontchartrain from the resorts on the south shore, where jazz was flourishing and evolving.

Virtually every jazz great of that time is purported to have traveled to Mandeville, then a thriving resort, to play the music that would soon take the world by storm. The likes of Kid Ory, Buck Johnson, Papa Celestin, George Lewis, Buddy Pettit and Louis Armstrong came here to play. They played not only for the crowds, but also for themselves, in an environment where they could experiment and let loose, refining their sound for the outside world.

Dew Drop lore claims that Armstrong would slip back into Mandeville during the 30s and 40s to escape the pressure of his growing global celebrity, to recharge his energy and to stay connected to his musical roots.

In the 1940s, African-American business began to succeed and the need for benvolent societies began to wane. The original community leaders who started the Dew Drop passed on and the building became almost abandoned, sitting unused for nearly 60 years.

In 2007, with impetus from the National Park Service, New Orleans Jazz Commission, the George Buck Foundation, and the City Of Mandeville, the venue was brought back into use and the sounds of traditional jazz were once again heard in the small music hall.

Today, proceeds from all events go to preserve and restore the hall and to support music education.

NORTHLAKE NATURE CENTER

30

The original habitat of the parish

23135 US-190 Mandeville, LA.
Tel: 985-626-1238
www.northlakenature.org
Open: dawn to dusk 7 days a week
Free entry

S t. Tammany Parish, just 45 minutes north of New Orleans, is one
of the fastest growing suburbs in the United States. It has seen ex-
plosive suburban growth in the past 40 years, yet the Northlake Nature
Center, located just east of the city of Mandeville, sits veiled from view,
preserving the natural feel of the area and transporting the visitor back
into the original habitat of the parish.

After parking your car in the small parking lot and walking a few feet
into the trees, you experience three different eco-systems: hardwood forests, pine-hardwood forests and pond swamp. These are all accessible by
modern boardwalks, with overlooks and interpretive signs along trails.
A new pavilion finished in 1998 gives entrée into this primitive world
and facilitates educational activities.

Trails cover nearly seven miles of the 400-acre preserve, bringing you
into the heart of a Louisiana wetland. There is a grove of southern mag-
nolias, a cypress/gum swamp and a pond created by beavers, including a
lodge visible from a scenic overlook. The spot teems with natural life: indigenous plants, animals and numerous bird species ranging from ducks
to songbirds and even a resident flock of wild turkeys. Bayou Castine
bounds the nature preserve on the west.

One of the most notable activities at the center each year is BirdFest.
This happens in spring, when Louisiana's geographic location on the
migration paths for birds returning to North America from wintering
in Mexico and South America lends itself to some of the finer birding
in the country.

There is also a human element present here. Archaeologists have
found remnants of a 700-year-old Acolipissa Native American population that called this site home. Ruins of a more recent vintage can be
seen in the guise of a golf course abandoned in the 1930s when its benefactor at the time, Governor Leche, was convicted and sent to prison.

The Northlake Nature Center was established in 1982 by a nonprof-
it organization to preserve, study and exhibit the natural and cultural
resources of Southeast Louisiana and the Florida Parishes (parishes just
north of New Orleans so named because they once belonged to the
Republic of Florida, a short-lived sovereign state).

31

ABITA MYSTERY HOUSE

*The most intriguing and provocative museum
in Louisiana*

*22275 LA-36 Highway
Abita Springs
Tel: 985-892-2624
www.abitamysteryhouse.com
Open: 10am–5pm daily*

Just off the center of Abita Springs, a former 1930s Standard Oil gas station houses the Abita Mystery House. This wonderland of eccentricity is the embodiment of the term 'American roadside attraction'. Located near the Tammany Trace trailhead in a sleepy, historic country town about 45 minutes north of New Orleans, the attraction all but defies description.

Areas open to visitors include the vintage gas station; the main exhibit building; an open-air section; a 90-year-old Creole cottage; and the House of Shards - a building festooned with broken mirrors, glass and pottery.

Within this tribute to kitsch, created by Abita artist John Preble, are more than a 1,000 found objects, homemade inventions and contraptions, push button activated displays, old arcade games, folk art, and what might simply be called employed junk. The Creole cottage now serves as a studio where artists create, invent and build the exhibits. In fact, visitors may even find children working on ideas that will one day appear in the museum. Management encourages this kind of participation. Some examples that give a flavor of the atmosphere of this found and assembled, ever-evolving 3D tapestry are: an Elvis shrine; a marble machine built of popsicle sticks; an Airstream trailer that a flying saucer seems to have crashed into; one-of-a-kind creatures with names like 'bassigator'; a 22-foot piece of folk art depicting a mythological half alligator, half fish creature created by Mr. Preble; and *River Road*, a 30-foot long satirical look in miniature at the small town culture along the river from Baton Rouge to New Orleans.

Preble, a longtime Abita resident, got the idea for his museum while traveling in New Mexico. After a lifetime spent gathering things, he turned his predilection for collecting into a curiosity shop that John Bullard, former curator of the New Orleans Museum of Art dubbed 'the most intriguing and provocative museum in Louisiana'. The Abita Mystery House is a constantly expanding universe of human whimsy. The place simply exudes fun and serves as an imagination lubricant for both young and old.

RONALD REAGAN STATUE

(32)

Largest Ronald Reagan statue in the world

Downtown Covington, Louisiana
About 35 miles north of New Orleans at the corner of N. New Hampshire and
E. Lockwood Streets at the trailhead of the Tammany Trace

In the heart of downtown Covington, at the center of parish government, stands the largest Ronald Reagan statue on earth. At almost 10 feet tall, it depicts the former president in a business suit, stood to attention, delivering a crisp military salute with that big Ronald Reagan signature smile.

Covington is a once sleepy country parish seat about 35 miles north of New Orleans that may initially seem an odd place to find the world's largest statue of President Ronald Reagan. After all, Reagan is honored all over the world with tributes: airports, streets, scholarship funds etc. Statues in places as far flung as Budapest, Poland, the Czech Republic, and Tbilisi (Georgia) are testament to the hold the 40th president of the United States has on the human imagination. In addition, Reagan never set foot in Covington and had no discernible connection to the town.

Yet on closer inspection, the parish, which is the most affluent and fastest growing in the state, has steadily become a Republican stronghold. Parish residents voted overwhelmingly for Reagan in his two presidential elections and his principles are revered among the populace.

The parish hasn't forgotten the Gipper.

In 2003, at the dedication of the street, a car pulled up and out stepped Patrick Taylor, one of the 400 richest men in the world and a personal friend of Ronald Reagan. Taylor vowed that he would build the largest statue in the world of Reagan after the former president passed away.

Mr. Taylor, an oil tycoon and well-known philanthropist, is the founder of the Louisiana TOPS program, which promises to pay the college tuition of all Louisiana high school students with good grades.

Taylor died only five months after President Reagan, but Taylor's wife Phyllis took over the job and delivered on her husband's promise. The statue went up in 2008 in the city center.

DR CHARLES SMITH AFRICAN AMERICAN HERITAGE MUSEUM

A showpiece of figures and statues with a purpose

S. Walnut Street, Hammond, Louisiana
Tel: 504-931-5744
Free entry
Visitors are welcome anytime. Call ahead to see if Dr. Smith will be on hand to give a tour

In Hammond, Louisiana, a veritable army of homemade concrete figures depicting every facet of African American history greets the visitor to the African American Heritage Museum and Black Veteran Archive of Dr. Charles Smith, a self-proclaimed doctor and retired Marine veteran of Vietnam.

Smith has transformed his modest home into a showpiece of figures and statues with a purpose: he hopes that after seeing his rambling heartfelt creations, folks will leave with a better understanding of issues that have, for better or worse, shaped the African American experience.

Dr. Smith chose concrete because he believed, "You should immortalize your work and termites can eat wood but they can't eat concrete."

Important figures in black history are here, such as Harriet Tubman, Sally Hemming, Maya Angelou and even a likeness of Denzel Washington in his role in the film *Glory*. But mostly, the sea of faces celebrated here are ordinary black citizens.

There are haunting faces on the house wall that depict the victims of Hurricane Katrina; symbolic figures in stereotypical poses with toothy grins, bug eyes and subservient gestures - images that were thrust upon African Americans throughout history. Many figures sport cameras that Smith scatters around the property to deter vandals.

Dr. Smith's work speaks for those who were once all but invisible in our society. His statues are "people standing up, holding their obituaries and ready to be seen by you and you and you."

Standing out from this crowd of faces are the numerous American flags waving in the wind; this is a whimsical expression but with a message.

Smith was moved to create his first museum by an inspiration he says came directly from God. That first museum in Aurora, Illinois, was eventually sold to the Kohler Foundation in order to spread his work out into prominent museums around the country. This allowed him to travel America, encouraging artists in places like Chicago, Simi Valley, Birmingham and New Orleans.

On a trip back south, he stopped in Hammond and saw the gravesite of Peter Hammond, the town's founder. On the tombstone were the names of Hammond's family along with a reference to a favorite "slave boy" who remains anonymous to this day - Smith has tried in vain to find any trace of his identity. Outraged at this, he decided to establish his next museum in Hammond.

LIGO

Measuring ripples in the fabric of space-time

19100 LIGO Lane, Livingston, Louisiana
Tel: 225-686-3100
www.ligo.caltech.edu/LA
Open: Every third Saturday 1pm–5pm
Entry fee: Public tours free of charge. Tours also available by special
arrangement

In a remote area of Livingston Parish, surrounded by a pine forest north of Lake Pontchartrain, LIGO (Laser Interferometer Gravitational-Wave Observatory) is one of America's most cutting-edge science and engineering facilities, administered by the National Science Foundation.

LIGO is home to one of two gravitational wave detectors (the other is 2162 miles away in Hanford, Washington) that are listening to "faint whispers of gravitational waves from the most energetic events in the universe" in an attempt to prove Einstein's prediction of their existence. According to the literature explaining this complex operation, such waves reach earth from cataclysmic events in deep space.

In order to hear the waves, highly sensitive instrumentation scans the heavens in incredible detail, measuring ripples in the fabric of space-time. Indeed, at 5:51 Eastern Daylight Time on September 14, 2015, the equipment detected a ping from the outer reaches of space, confirming Einstein's 1916 prediction pertaining to his famous general theory of relativity, thereby proving the existence of gravitational waves.

On December 26, 2015, the detectors received a second, more robust signal from two black holes in their final orbit and their subsequent coalescence into a single entity. The event measured on that day occurred over a billion years ago.

LIGO is in a remote area of the region; until the momentous discoveries of 2015, most people were not even aware of its existence. Since those discoveries of worldwide import, it has again faded from general public consciousness.

What most people don't know is that the Science Education Center attached to LIGO has an exhibit that is open to the public free of charge. Every third Saturday of the month, visitors are welcome to the facility's mini museum, which contains 50 interactive science exhibits with scientists on hand to answer questions. These open houses at the facility are designed to inspire the scientist in every visitor.

The facility is also open by appointment to teachers, students and educational groups throughout the year.

NOTES

ACKNOWLEDGEMENTS

Our thanks to:

American Italian Cultural Center, Stanley Amerski, Tom Amoss, Alexander Barkoff, Larry Beron, Yvonne Blount, Richard Boyd, Bonnie Broel, Marcus Bronson, Christy Brown, Brad Bryant, Sarah Burnette, Joe Cabral, Richard Campanella, Kristin Core, Cancy DuBos, Heather Englehart, Randy Ernst, Mike Fedor, Gina Ferrara, German –American Cultural Center, Leon Greenblatt, Ride Hamilton, Jeb Harrison, Irish Cultural Museum, Lynne Jensen, Pat Jolly, Bill Kearney, Paul LaNoue, Susan Larson, Remy Lazare, Mary Ledbetter, Rodney Lewis, Angus Lind, King Logan, Los Islenos Heritage & Cultural Center, Eddie Mack, Howard Margot, Delaney Martin, Heidi Melancon, Philip Melancon, Middle American Research Institute(Tulane University), Geoff Munsterman, Ogden Museum of Southern Art, Amber Qureshi, Aryna Rarinushka, Matt Scallan, Edgar Mauri Sierra, Taylor Sheperd, Rebecca Smith, Jason Songe, Swan River Yoga Studios, John Sudsbury, The Historic New Orleans Collection, Elizabeth Thompson, Robert Thompson, Jonathon Traviesa, John Travis, Janis Turk, John Verano, Ronnie Virgets, Gary Williams, Michael Williams, Chris Wiltz

PHOTOGRAPHY CREDITS

Paul Lanoue: All photos but...

Jonathan Traviesa: 98 Racehorse Graves, 99 Seven Sisters Oak,100 Camp Parapet, 102 Ochsner Dimes, 103 Baldwin Wood Pumps, 104 Cowan Man, 108 Music Box Village, 109 M. S.Rau Secret Room, 112 Port of New Orleans Place, 113 LIGO, 116 Creole Castle, 117 World's Fair photos

Elizabeth Garcia-107 Nicholas Cage Grave

Pat Jolly: 105 Backstreet Museum

Edgar Mauri Sierra: 106 Everette Maddox Poetry Reading

Marcus Bronson: 96 Rex Den

Chris Champagne: 79 Irish Channel Tiny Museum, 114 Hank Was Here, 120 Bevolo Lighting

The Historic New Orleans Collection (THNOC): 46 J&M Studio and 50 United Fruit Building

Maps: **Cyrille Suss** - Layout design: **Coralie Cintrat** - Layout: **Iperbole** - Proofreading: **Matt Gay and Eleni Salemi**

© JONGLEZ 2018
Registration of copyright: May 2018 – Edition: 02
ISBN: 978-2-36195-168-9
Printed in Bulgaria by Dedrax